# Popes, Emperors, and Elephants

# Popes, Emperors, and Elephants

## THE FIRST THOUSAND YEARS OF CHRISTIAN CULTURE

ROY PEACHEY

Angelico Press

First published in the USA
by Angelico Press 2021
Copyright © Roy Peachey 2021

For information, address:
Angelico Press, Ltd.
169 Monitor St.
Brooklyn, NY 11222
www.angelicopress.com

978-1-62138-699-5 pbk
978-1-62138-701-5 cloth
978-1-62138-700-8 ebook

Book and cover design
by Michael Schrauzer

AMDG

If history records good things of good men, the thoughtful hearer is encouraged to imitate what is good: or if it records evil of wicked men, the devout, religious listener or reader is encouraged to avoid all that is sinful and perverse and to follow what he knows to be good and pleasing to God.

Saint Bede the Venerable
*A History of the English Church and People*

# CONTENTS

# CHAPTER 1

## *Trying to Find a Beginning*

LET'S START AT THE VERY BEGINNING: A VERY good place to start, according to Maria in *The Sound of Music*. Unfortunately, it's not always that easy, especially for historians. Historians aren't very good at beginnings. The further back we go the less evidence we have. History becomes story. Facts dissolve into myth.

And there's another problem. If we want to understand the world we live in we need to decide which parts of history to study. The history of America? The history of the West? Or even the history of the whole world?

So, let's start somewhere else. Let's start with history itself. Such a simple word—such a complicated concept. The word "history" comes from a Greek word meaning "story" among other things. But, of course, history isn't any old story. It's a true story. Or a story that tries to draw as close to the truth as it can. But, as with all good stories, history can be told in many different ways and so there are many different types of history, just as there are many different types of story.

The Greeks believed that history was cyclical; it went round and round in circles. They thought it was something like a Ferris wheel: cultures and societies moved very slowly; they gradually came to a high point and then they declined. According to the Greeks, history was doomed to repeat itself.

But not all societies thought like that. The Jews had a radically different view of history which they passed on to Christians. They believed that history was linear, that it had a start and moved forward in a straight line. Now this might seem blindingly obvious to you but that's because you have grown up in a society that has been shaped by a Judaeo-Christian (in other words, a Jewish and Christian) understanding of history.

The Greeks had a very great respect for history—one of their nine muses, Clio, was the goddess of history—but their view of history was not ours. Take Herodotus, who has been called the father of history, as an example. He wrote a book called *The Histories* in the fifth century BC. Right at the start of his book he explained that "many states that were once great have now become small; those that were great in my time were small before. Knowing therefore that human prosperity never continues in the same place, I shall mention both alike." In other words, countries prosper and then decline and then rise again. History goes round on a wheel. Later in the book he made the point even more clearly by putting words into the mouth of a man called Croesus, who was trying to persuade Cyrus, the king of Persia, to keep a foreign army out of his territory: "I must first teach you this: men's fortunes are on a wheel, which in its turning does not allow the same man to prosper forever."

The key word in Greek is κύκλος, which means "wheel." It's the word from which we get our word "cycle." The idea that our fortunes are on a wheel has been very popular over the years, but it is a terribly depressing idea. Just when life seems be going well, the wheel turns and we tumble into disaster. Herodotus spelt this out by giving these words to a man called Solon: "It is necessary to see how the end of every affair turns out, for the god promises fortune to many people and then utterly ruins them."

In this view of the world the gods are against us or, at the very least, they can't be completely trusted. That was a view that the first Christians challenged with all their might. Instead of fatalism, they spoke about hope. Instead of disaster, they spoke about faith. Instead of ruin, they spoke about love. It was a revolutionary message.

There were some ideas that the early Christians refused to take from the Greeks but they didn't reject the Greek world entirely. Like bees flying from flower to flower, they took whatever was good from Greek culture and made it their own. To understand how this worked, we need to dip into a couple of empires that lasted a very long time. The Glory that was Greece (as some people call it) lasted for over 1000 years, from the time of the first Olympiad in 776 BC until the closing of the great school of Athens in AD 529. And the Romans were around for even longer, from something like 750 BC to AD 1453, which is not the date you'll find in every history textbook, for reasons we'll consider later.

We certainly can't cover a thousand years in any detail, so let's have a quick look at the Greeks' main achievements instead. Then let's consider the Romans' debt to the Greeks. After that we can return to the moment when a new force entered the world, a force that changed history forever.

# CHAPTER 2

## *What Was So Great About Greece?*

THE ANCIENT GREEKS MADE BREAKTHROUGHS in all sorts of different areas: in mathematics, astronomy, drama, poetry, and philosophy. Especially philosophy. The Greeks were great thinkers and the greatest among them were Socrates, who wrote no books at all, Plato (his pupil) who wrote lots, and Aristotle (Plato's pupil) who wrote even more. It is no exaggeration to say that Socrates, Plato, and Aristotle were the fathers of philosophy. What they said and wrote shaped the way people thought about some of the really big questions in life for the next two and a half thousand years.

We cannot do their work justice in a little book like this, so let's focus on just one question they raised: how to be happy.

We'll focus on Aristotle who wrote about *eudaimonia*, which is sometimes translated as "happiness" but which is more accurately translated as "human flourishing." Aristotle wanted to find out what makes us truly happy, what gives us lasting happiness. To find an answer to that question, he took a step back and asked what the *ergon* (the function, task, or work) of a human being is. Just like flautists, sculptors, or craftsmen (to use his examples) who have a clear job to do and are fulfilled when they do that job well, all humans have a job to do too. So, what is our main job in life? It is to exercise our soul's faculties in conformity with excellence or virtue, to use Aristotle's own precise language. To put it simply, being happy is something we *do*.

Happiness comes from living well, Aristotle argued, but too often we think that happiness comes from external circumstances: how much money we have; how great our friends are; where we go on holiday. Not so, Aristotle said. He claimed that what people often have as their goals in life—wealth or health, for example—are not what give us ultimate happiness. What gives us ultimate happiness is embedding the virtues in our lives and that takes a long time. In fact, "to be happy takes a complete lifetime," he wrote.

But what did he mean by the virtues, that word I have now dropped in twice? He meant things like courage, truthfulness, modesty, and generosity. He also wrote about some virtues that may be less familiar to us. Virtues like temperance, for example. Sometimes the easiest way to understand what Aristotle meant is to look at the examples he gives of related vices. Courage, for example, is a great virtue. The related vices both relate to fear. If we have too much fear we become cowardly and if we have too little fear we become rash. But if we face the world as it really is, we know that we have to be courageous because it is neither a completely safe place nor a place that is filled with dangers at every turn.

But let's get back to temperance. The related vices are self-indulgence (simply gorging ourselves on any pleasant experience, whether it be food, drink, or anything else that makes us feel good) and its opposite, a lack of feeling (when we become numbed to pleasures entirely). Temperance is knowing how to enjoy life by not going to either extreme. What does that mean in practice? Let me give an example that you won't find in Aristotle's *Nicomachean Ethics* (the book in which he set out his ideas about happiness, human flourishing, and the virtues).

When I was a child I went to Turkey on a school trip. Every shop along the harbor front offered free samples of Turkish Delight. Because I did not have the virtue of temperance, I visited every shop I could find and tried out more and more free samples. For a while it was great. I love Turkish Delight! But before long I started to feel very sick indeed. Aristotle would not have been surprised. He knew that eating a few pieces of Turkish Delight is much more pleasurable than stuffing yourself with as many pieces as you can lay your hands on. That is what he meant by actively exercising our soul's faculties in conformity with excellence or virtue: there comes a time when we need to stop eating Turkish Delight. Happiness comes from *doing* the right thing.

Of course, this is a very limited example and Aristotle wrote a lot more profoundly than I have here, but it gives you a taste of Greek philosophy and how wonderful it was. Later Christian thinkers seized on the ideas of Aristotle, Plato, and Socrates and developed them further. The most important of these thinkers was Saint Thomas Aquinas. If you ever get a chance to study his philosophy, please do because it is truly wonderful!

Greek philosophy wasn't just about ideas. The way in which Socrates, Plato, and Aristotle did their work was also important. Philosophy for them was not a subject to be studied in school; it was a way of life. Socrates used to walk around the public squares of Athens and chat to people. He asked them apparently simple questions and then developed their ideas by asking more questions. We now speak of the Socratic Method as an important feature of education. A good teacher can help his or her students discover the truth through careful questioning. A good student can learn a great deal by asking and answering questions thoughtfully. Asking the right questions and developing thoughtful answers is a great way of getting to the truth. That is why Plato's books are full of conversations. That's one reason why they are a real pleasure to read. For Socrates, Plato, and Aristotle, philosophy was part of life. They certainly didn't think that the only place we can learn is in a classroom.

The Greeks gave us philosophy as we understand it today but they weren't just great thinkers; they also wrote wonderful plays. The earliest tragedies were written by Greek dramatists like Aeschylus, Euripides, and Sophocles. When I was fifteen I spent a couple of weeks at an Ancient Greek summer school, at the end of which the students and a few of the teachers staged one of these tragedies. In Ancient Greek. I understood about three words.

In fact, come to think of it, that's probably an exaggeration.

But even though I understood only one or two words, I was still bowled over by the experience, which is pretty surprising because not a lot happens in Greek tragedies. Most of the action takes place off stage. There aren't many characters and they all talk a lot. (Actually there's one exception to that rule and I'll mention him in a minute.)

Nevertheless, I sat through over two hours of Greek drama, not understanding the language and not knowing much about the plot, and I still enjoyed it. Why? Because Greek tragedy is written in verse. And what verse! It was more like sitting through a concert, a concert in which jazz meets hip hop meets Stravinsky, because the Greeks weren't just masters of philosophy; they were also masters of poetry and drama. Greek poetry is like nothing you've ever heard before; it's beautiful and it's rhythmic. Just imagine what an experience I'd have had if I'd understood what they were talking about!

Greek tragedies, like the Greek view of history, could be very bleak. The first Greek Tragedy I saw was *Prometheus Bound* by Aeschylus. After stealing fire from the gods and giving it to mankind, Prometheus is chained to a rock as a punishment from Zeus and that is where he stays throughout the whole play! All that happens in the play is that various Titans and gods try to persuade Prometheus to give in to the will of Zeus. Prometheus refuses and so at the end of the play he is swallowed up by the underworld. It is not an action-packed adventure but that doesn't matter because what Aeschylus was really interested in was the clash of wills between Prometheus and Zeus. It was a psychological drama written in beautiful poetry. It was a story that has continued to haunt people's imaginations for hundreds and hundreds of years.

It is not strictly relevant to the drama but you might also be interested to hear that Aeschylus died in a rather unusual way according to Valerius Maximus, a Roman author: "Leaving the walls of the town where he was staying, he sat down in a sunny spot. An eagle carrying a tortoise was above him. Deceived by the gleam of his hairless skull, it dashed the tortoise against it, as though it were a stone, in order to feed on the flesh of the broken animal." And that was the end of poor Aeschylus. History doesn't record what happened to the tortoise.

The genius of the Greeks didn't stop with philosophy, poetry, or drama (each of which words, incidentally, entered our language from Greek). You don't need to do much Math before you come across Greek letters: π for a start (or 3.1415926 etc. if you prefer it as a number). The Greeks were amazing mathematicians. Perhaps the most impressive of all were Archimedes, who discovered (while getting into a bath) that a floating body displaces its own weight in liquid, and Euclid, who is known as the Father of Geometry and whose baths haven't entered the history books.

The only significant gap in their work was that they didn't have a symbol for zero and you'd be surprised how much that matters in math. Fortunately, Islamic scholars brought the concept of zero from India and the subject hasn't looked back since.

The Greeks also made some scientific advances. The key players here were Leucippus and Democritus, who came up with the first atomic theories (the idea that all matter is made up of tiny atoms); Hipparchus, who was an early and highly influential astronomer; and Ptolemy, who was a geographer as well as a mathematician and astronomer. However, despite their many successes the Greeks didn't go on to develop a fully scientific understanding of the world. We will explore why this was the case in a later chapter.

One of the dangers with lists of names, like the ones we have given here, is that they tend to suggest that everything happened at once. But the Glory that was Greece lasted for a very long time. *The Iliad* and *The Odyssey* (two great poems by Homer) were written so long ago that we're not really sure when they were composed (the eighth century BC seems a fair guess) but other influential writers like Galen and Plutarch (a doctor and a historian) were working as late as the second century AD. In other words, a thousand years later.

Another danger is that we ignore what the Greeks actually wrote. We shouldn't make this mistake because many of their books are surprisingly readable. Shakespeare certainly thought so. That's why he took many of his stories (and some of his descriptions) straight from Plutarch. Homer too has been incredibly influential, so let's pause for a moment and look at *The Iliad* and *The Odyssey*. These two epic poems center on the Trojan wars. You may well be familiar with the story of Helen, who ran away with Paris of Troy, leaving her husband, Menelaus, the King of Sparta. The Greeks then gathered an enormous fleet of ships that sailed to Troy and besieged the city for many years, eventually winning the war by leaving a great wooden horse (inside which some Greek soldiers were hiding) and pretending to withdraw from the battlefield.

What surprises many people is how little of this great story is covered in Homer's *Iliad*. Homer could assume that his listeners knew the story already, so he concentrated on just one small part of the tale, focusing on the characters of Achilles and Hector. It is a great poem about war, anger, and jealousy. It is written in wonderful poetry and with great narrative drive. But it doesn't cover much of the story.

Homer's other great poem, *The Odyssey*, is a sequel but it too leaves much of the story untold. This time Homer focused on Odysseus and his long, long, long journey home. In some ways, *The Odyssey* is the more accessible of the two poems because it is more like the sort of fantasy adventure stories we are used to today. On his way back to his faithful wife, Penelope, Odysseus meets many strange (and dangerous) characters. He is shipwrecked, has half his crew turned into sheep, and even visits the underworld. It is a story made for Hollywood. Except, of course, that wasn't Homer's intention at all. *The Odyssey* and *The Iliad* were probably meant to be *heard*. We now live in an extremely visual culture and are no longer very good at listening, but for those who can recover the skill there are very great rewards.

Our world grew out of the great cultures of Ancient Greece, Rome, and Israel, but before we get onto the

Romans and the Israelites, I need to finish my story about Greek tragedy. Two years after I sat through a Greek play without understanding a word of it, I found myself performing in one. This would have been pretty daunting had I not been playing the part of Pylades in a play called the *Choephori* by Euripides. I had three lines. It's the shortest speaking part in all Greek tragedy and even I could manage three lines.

# CHAPTER 3

## Julius Caesar and the First Roman Emperors

ONE OF THE PROBLEMS WITH STUDYING THE Roman Empire is that we think we know all about it. So, here's a simple question to start us off: what was the capital of the Roman Empire? Seems obvious, doesn't it? Rome, by definition, was the capital of the Roman Empire. If that was your answer then you were right. Partly right. Because the answer's also Constantinople (now called Istanbul), Ravenna (in northern Italy), and even Trier (which is now in Germany but was then in Gaul). I could go on. At different times, all these places were the capital of the Roman Empire.

One of the great things about history is that it constantly surprises us. We think we've got hold of the past and then some inconvenient facts jump up and force us to look again at what's wriggling in our hands.

So, some inconvenient facts:

1. After AD 324 the Empire had two capitals: Rome and Constantinople.

2. At the end of the third century, there were, in effect, five capitals: Rome, Milan, Trier, Izmit (in what we now call Turkey), and Sremska Mitrovica (in what we now call Serbia).

3. For the first half of the fifth century, it had two capitals: Ravenna and Constantinople.

All of which suggests that the Roman Empire is a lot more complicated than we usually think. If we are to get a grip on the empire we need to be aware of the fact that it lasted for a lot longer than most people appreciate and that there was much more to the Roman Empire than Rome.

However, we also need to remember that Rome *was* hugely important. It was a great symbol as well as a great place. The word for China in Chinese is Zhongguo (中国), which means Middle Kingdom. For hundreds of years the Chinese saw themselves as being at the center of the world. The same was true of the Romans. Their world extended as far as Egypt to the South and Ultima Thule to the North, but the center was clearly Rome.

The early emperors knew that they had to have a firm power base in Rome. They knew that they had to spend big money on big building projects in Rome. They had to put on lavish entertainments in Rome and keep the Roman citizens and Roman Senate happy. When the emperor Constantine moved the capital to Constantinople in the fourth century AD it was a huge symbolic gesture. And when a hundred years after that Rome was all but destroyed by the Visigoths it was a massive symbolic blow, even though Rome was no longer the center of political power. But more on all that later in the book.

So, let's go back in time and ask where Rome came from. As early as around 1000 BC there had been tiny villages where the city of Rome was later built, but we can only meaningfully speak of Rome itself from c. 600 BC when the Forum was laid out. (The Forum was a large public square where legal, political, and religious business took place, as well as a certain amount of buying and selling. And that little c. before the date, by the way, stands for *circa*, a Latin word meaning "around" or "about.") For the next 400 years the power of Rome kept growing, especially after the Romans defeated their main rivals, the people of Carthage in what is now called Tunisia, in the third century BC. From that point onward the Romans controlled much of the Mediterranean and the fertile land around it. The Romans controlled the Mediterranean but they saw themselves as kings of the world. One of their poets, a man called Ovid, put it like this: "The land of other nations has a fixed boundary; the space of Rome is the space of the world." (*Gentibus est aliis tellus data limite certo; Romanae spatium est urbis et orbis idem.*) This was the world which Julius Caesar burst into.

For hundreds of years Rome was a republic. In other words, it was ruled not by an emperor or king but by the people as represented in the Senate. There was no sense of democracy as we know it today (or as the Athenians knew it in Greece) but there was a clear sense that power should not be concentrated in the hands of one man.

However, one man did emerge as a powerful leader after a period of civil wars. Julius Caesar was a soldier who, along with Pompey and Crassus, was the most important man in Rome during the last days of the Republic. Julius Caesar was a consul (an important Roman politician) but his real power came from being a highly successful general. Being posted to Gaul offered him the chance of glory and power. At that time, Rome controlled the southern part of Gaul. Julius Caesar managed to take over most of the rest of Gaul in a series of bloody battles that left over a million people dead. The Battle of Bibracte in 58 BC has been described as "one of the bloodiest afternoons in history"; there were more casualties than on the first day of the Battle of the Somme in World War I, which is remembered today as one of the most terrible days in the history of modern warfare.

Julius Caesar was a very successful soldier but he was also a shrewd politician. He knew that, being away from Rome for many years, he could very easily be forgotten. He made sure he wasn't forgotten by writing seven volumes about the Gallic War (*De Bello Gallico*). In this book he wrote about himself in the third person, giving the impression that he was an all-knowing writer and an all-knowing general. The reality was slightly different, of course. Though hugely successful in Gaul, he wasn't able to bring Britain into the Roman Empire. That happened during the reign of the Emperor Claudius almost a hundred years later.

Nonetheless, Julius Caesar was extremely powerful. During his time in Gaul, he built up a very powerful network of friends and advisors. Above all, he made sure that his army was on his side. What he was preparing for was a march on Rome. At that time, generals had a lot of power over their troops, but they were supposed to leave their armies behind when they returned to Rome. The Roman Senate guarded their privileges jealously and did not want to be bullied into action by generals and their soldiers. The crunch point came when Julius Caesar disobeyed the Senate and marched his army as far as the Rubicon, a river that is in modern-day Italy but which then marked the boundary between Cisalpine Gaul and Italy. The moment Julius Caesar crossed the Rubicon he was, in effect, declaring war.

His main enemy in Rome was a man called Pompey who moved eastward, abandoning Italy. Julius Caesar moved very quickly after him which meant that the civil war was fought mainly in Greece. When the battles went badly for him there, Pompey fled to Egypt where he was beheaded by Ptolemy XIII, who then gave the head to Julius Caesar. The other crucial event in Egypt was that Julius Caesar fell in love with Cleopatra who was Ptolemy's wife and sister. Since she was determined to meet this powerful Roman general, Cleopatra managed to get herself smuggled into the palace.

You might have heard that she did this by being rolled up in a carpet and then carried in under the noses of Ptolemy's guards but this story is based on a mistranslation. She was actually smuggled into the palace in a kit bag (which is still a remarkable way of introducing yourself to a visiting dignitary!).

This period of Roman history was rather chaotic. Even though Pompey had been defeated, Julius Caesar had to carry on fighting, pursuing his enemies as far as Spain. Equally important was the fact that, with an army at his back, he managed to persuade the Senate to elect him as dictator for a limited number of years and then declared himself dictator for life in 44 BC, thereby becoming, in effect, the first Roman emperor.

This was a deeply unpopular move among many in the Senate, but Caesar seemed to get away with it at first. He reformed the calendar (mainly because the year was ten days short!). This meant adding a leap year for a start. Then the month called "Quintilis" was renamed as "Julius" (or July) in honor of Julius Caesar. A few years later another month, "Sextilis," was also renamed, becoming "Augustus" (or August) for Augustus Caesar.

Among his other reforms, Julius Caesar increased the number of magistrates in the city and so expanded the Senate. He also became recognized as a god. Being told they had to worship the Roman emperor was one of the major problems the early Christians faced, but pagan Romans were surprisingly indifferent to this move. What really mattered to them was the horrifying idea that Julius Caesar might want to be a king.

The Roman Republic was extremely proud of the fact that it had got rid of kings years before, so when Julius Caesar started to dress like one—wearing a purple cloak, long red boots, and a laurel wreath to cover his bald head—they became worried and annoyed. It was no great surprise that he was assassinated on the Ides of March (15$^{th}$ March) 44 BC by a group of plotters that included Mark Antony, who was also a general and politician, and his former friend Brutus.

The Republic had been saved, or so it seemed. In reality, a precedent had been set. Mark Antony dealt ruthlessly with his opponents (like the great orator Cicero, who was beheaded) and looked set to become a new dictator, which is why the Senate sent Julius Caesar's nephew and adopted heir, Octavian, to stop him. To everyone's surprise the two men joined forces and ruled the empire for another twelve years, along with another general called Lepidus. Octavian was only nineteen at the time.

Eventually, Mark Antony and Octavian fell out. They fought until Mark Antony was defeated for good at the naval battle of Actium. He and his lover, Cleopatra, committed suicide leaving Octavian in sole command of the empire. From then on there was no looking back. The Republic was over and the Empire was there to stay.

A few years later Octavian took the title of Augustus (or Emperor). He later added a few other titles like *princeps* (or First Citizen) and *Pontifex Maximus* (High Priest) and ruled until his death in 14 BC, having ruled for longer than any other emperor managed over the succeeding centuries. He was then succeeded by his adopted son, Tiberius. From that point onward (until the emperor Constantine converted to Christianity) the emperors, dead and alive, were worshiped as gods. Their heads appeared on coins. Their busts were placed in temples. Failure to burn incense or make sacrifices to them was a crime that was punished by death.

From that time until the end of the Roman Empire almost one and a half thousand years later, the emperors ruled supreme. The relationship between the emperors and the Senate was not the same as the relationship between the President of the United States and Congress. In effect, the emperors had total power backed up by their control of the armies. In the early first century AD the emperors had something like a quarter of a million soldiers stationed around the empire. That is why most of them, with the interesting exception of Hadrian, felt that they could stay in Rome almost all the time. They could leave the fighting to others and, if they did travel, they tended not to stay away too long (though Tiberius did retire to the island of Capri for the last twelve years of his life).

But the emperors didn't all behave in the same way. Some, like Nero and Caligula, are remembered for their cruelty and wickedness, while others, like Marcus Aurelius, are remembered for their great learning. All of them were powerful and ruthless in dealing with their enemies. Theirs was the world into which Jesus of Nazareth was born.

# CHAPTER 4

## Judaism and the Roman Empire

THE WORLD INTO WHICH JESUS WAS BORN was one in which the demands of distant Roman emperors could force heavily pregnant women to trek miles so that they could be registered in a Roman census; a world in which Judaea was a province ruled by the Romans; a world in which Greek, thanks to the conquests of Alexander the Great, was the favored language of the educated elite. Most of the Old Testament is written in Hebrew but there are two books (The Wisdom of Solomon and 2 Maccabees) that were originally written in Greek. What's more, by the time of Jesus the whole of the Hebrew Bible (the Christian Old Testament) had been translated into Greek (in a version known as the Septuagint).

Neither the Jews nor the early Christians (many of whom were, of course, Jewish) had an entirely happy time in the Roman Empire. In AD 66, for example, a rebellion began in Jerusalem against the Romans. Four years later the Romans destroyed much of the city, including the Temple itself, in a furious act of vengeance. The war began when the Roman governor, Florus, who had been appointed by the emperor Nero, ordered the inhabitants of Jerusalem to process out of the city to greet two cohorts of Roman soldiers. As insults were thrown, the soldiers lashed out, striking the Jews with their clubs and trampling them under the feet of their horses. Florus then gave orders to his soldiers to kill all the Jews they met as they marauded through the market area. A short time later 3,600 Jews—men, women, and children—were dead.

Terrible as these events were, the situation eventually became much worse. In AD 70 a Roman army, led by Titus, son of the Roman emperor, laid siege to the city in an attempt to starve the inhabitants into submission. The suffering that followed was intense. Thousands died of starvation and anyone who was caught fleeing the city was publicly crucified. Inside the city, people resorted to desperate measures to stay alive, searching the sewers for old cow dung to eat and chewing on whatever they could find, including belts, shoes and tufts of withered grass.

Titus then battered his way through the outer walls, forcing the defenders ever deeper into the city until they took refuge in the Temple, which eventually caught fire, allowing the Roman soldiers to sweep in unopposed: "While the Temple blazed, the victors plundered everything that fell in their way and slaughtered wholesale all who were caught. No pity was shown for age, no reverence for rank; children and greybeards, laity and priests, alike were massacred."

This description, and much of the information we have about the Jewish rebellion and the destruction of the Temple, comes from a man called Josephus. Josephus is often described as a Jewish historian, but forget any idea of a respectable academic working in a quiet library. Josephus was a much more complicated figure than that. Born and bred in Jerusalem, he joined the rebellion against the Romans in AD 66 and was placed in charge of the defense of Galilee. However, he was not a great soldier and was captured by the Romans. Cannily the Romans didn't execute him but, as we would say today, they decided to turn him.

He was sent to Rome, given somewhere to live in the city, and granted a state pension. He then settled down to write a series of books about Jews and Judaism.

Josephus undoubtedly had a comfortable life but a troubled conscience. He claimed that he had changed sides because of dreams sent by God, but the truth was that he was now in the pay of the Romans and had to keep his new masters happy. That is why he traveled to Jerusalem when it was under siege; his task was to persuade the defenders to surrender.

Josephus was certainly not a neutral witness—he was deeply compromised by his new position in Rome—but he did know Jerusalem, he did understand Judaism, and he did witness many of the terrible events he described. His books are, therefore, extremely useful historical sources, as long as we read them with a certain amount of caution. We also need to remember that the story of unbearable conflict between the Jews and the Romans is only part of the story. There were other rebellions but none so devastating as the one Josephus described. And there were times when Rome and Jerusalem got on reasonably well. We should not assume that conflict was inevitable.

In fact, Roman violence against a foreign religion is, in some ways, quite surprising because the Romans were generally rather good at dealing with foreign religions. When you conquer an empire as large as the Romans conquered you come face to face with a lot of different gods. The Romans could have created havoc by trying to suppress the worship of Zeus and Athena, of Mithras and Isis, but they didn't. They simply incorporated them into their own **pantheon**.* They took these foreign gods as their own.

As often as not, this simply meant that they saw these foreign gods as manifestations of their own familiar **deities**. So, in Britain, for example, archaeologists

* Any words printed in **bold** are defined in the Glossary (Appendix B).

have found an inscription to "the god Maponus Apollo." Apollo was originally a Greek God who was then adopted by the Romans, and Maponus was a British Celtic god. For the Romans Maponus and Apollo were simply different names for the same god.

We can see the same idea expressed in the days of the week. What the French call *mardi* (the day of Mars) the English call Tuesday (the day of Tiw). Again, to the Romans there was no difference between Mars and Tiw.

So, what was different about Judaism and Christianity? Why didn't they fit in? First and foremost, Jews and Christians are monotheists. They believe in one God. Rather inconveniently for the Romans, Jews and Christians didn't want their God to be incorporated into the great Olympian team. Their God was the only God and the Romans found this idea difficult to stomach.

The second reason Jews and Christians didn't fit in was that they refused to do what the Romans regarded as their civic duty: make sacrifices to the Roman gods (including the emperor-gods). This made them politically suspect. If you couldn't rely on Christians and Jews to sacrifice to the gods in public, could you trust them to defend your empire? It is not surprising that many of the earliest Christian martyrs were Roman soldiers.

However, there were also some key differences between the Jews and the Christians. It wasn't until about AD 310 (and, arguably, not even then) that Christianity started to rely on the Roman Empire for support. The size and stability of the Roman Empire certainly helped Christianity to spread but Christianity never relied on the empire to help it spread the Gospel.

The Irish and the Ethiopians were converted to Christianity quite early on, for example, and neither Ireland nor Ethiopia was ever part of the Roman Empire. Judaism, by contrast, was much more closely associated with politics. The kingdom of Israel was absolutely central to Jewish identity. So, even though the Jews had been defeated in battle many times before, the conquest of Israel by the Romans in 63 BC was an utter disaster. The Temple—the site of God's very presence—had been defiled by the Babylonians when they forced the Jews into exile in the sixth century BC and the Jewish authorities were determined that it shouldn't happen again, even if that meant collaborating politically with the Roman regime.

However, you don't need to read much in the Gospels to realize that many Jews at the time of Jesus were longing for the day when they could get rid of the Romans. When the rebellion came, though, it was a disaster. After destroying the Temple and much of Jerusalem, the Romans banned Jews from entering Jerusalem except on one day a year. Indeed, if you go to Rome you can still see carvings of Roman soldiers looting holy items from the Temple on Titus's Arch, the triumphal arch built to celebrate their victory.

If that wasn't bad enough, things got worse after another rebellion, the Bar-Kochba Rebellion, in AD 135. This too was brutally crushed and Jews were banned from entering Jerusalem at all. There were already many Jewish communities across Europe and Asia but the Diaspora, the dispersal of Jewish communities across the known world, picked up its pace after the failed rebellions. While some Jews remained in Israel others traveled as far as Spain in the West, what we now call Russia in the North, into North Africa and as far east as India. In fact, some of the most important Jewish communities after AD 70 were not in Europe at all, but in Babylon (modern-day Iraq).

Judaism was changed forever by the failed rebellions. Since temple worship and the kingdom of Israel could no longer be at the heart of Judaism, synagogues and rabbis became increasingly important. Jews tended either to become assimilated into the cultures in which they found refuge or they kept their heads down, living in close-knit communities and preserving their religious beliefs and traditions. Though there were some high-profile exceptions, Jews were often mocked or ignored by the Romans after the fall of Jerusalem, as long as they didn't cause any political trouble.

There were also some unintended consequences of the rebellions. In their determination to stamp out the new religion, the Romans built their own temples on three key sites: in Nazareth, Bethlehem, and Jerusalem. The Romans wanted to wipe out any memory of the religions that had caused them such trouble; as it was, they actually marked the site of the Holy Places for future generations. When Christianity eventually became the official religion of the Roman Empire, it was a relatively straightforward task to build churches in the places where Jesus had lived, preached, and worked his miracles. The Romans had told the Christians, who had been scattered all round the known world, exactly where to look.

# CHAPTER 5

## *Christianity in the Roman Empire*

CHRISTIANITY EMERGED INTO A WORLD that was dominated by the Romans and indebted to the Greeks, but it was born in Israel and spread from there. What we now call Israel was at that time a Roman province, ruled by a Roman governor, Pontius Pilate. So, let's have a closer look at the man who eventually sent Jesus to his death. Pilate was governor of Judaea from AD 26 to 36 and during that time there were a number of problems caused by his stubbornness and lack of sympathy for the people he ruled. On one occasion he took money from the Temple to pay for an aqueduct. Another time he brought military standards decorated with the image of the emperor-god into Jerusalem with apparently no understanding of the offence they would cause. Having caused these problems, he quickly turned to violence to enforce his will on the people.

Agrippa I, king of Judaea, described him in a letter as "vindictive, with a furious temper" and Josephus tells us that Pilate sent soldiers "armed but disguised in civilian clothes, with orders not to use their swords, but to beat any rioters with cudgels.... Large numbers of the Jews perished, some from the blows which they received, others trodden to death by their companions in the ensuing flight. Cowed by the fate of the victims, the multitude was reduced to silence." This is the context we need if we are to understand Pilate's cowardly behavior when Jesus was brought before him. Having caused several riots already, he didn't want another one, especially one concerning a Jewish rabbi whose teaching was of little interest to him.

Pontius Pilate had all the real power in Judaea (as long as he did what the Roman emperor wanted) but he didn't rule alone. The Romans were quite happy to allow local leaders to have some limited control over parts of their provinces, believing that rebellions were less likely if local leaders ruled on their behalf. That is why they allowed Herod Antipas, son of Herod the Great, to rule over Galilee as a tetrarch, or local leader.

Herod was also more concerned with his own position than he was with doing the right thing. That is why he had John the Baptist beheaded for protesting against Herod's decision to divorce his wife and marry Herodias instead. This upset his own subjects, who objected to the fact that Herodias had been the wife of Herod's half-brother, and Aretas IV, who was king of a nearby kingdom. Herod's first wife was King Aretas's daughter so he later invaded Herod's territory in an act of revenge.

When Jesus was arrested Pontius Pilate and Herod tried to pass the buck to each other. Pilate saw him first but then figured he could wriggle out of the inconvenience by passing him on to Herod. Herod was clearly fascinated by Jesus but passed him back to Pilate when he realized that Jesus wasn't going to perform miracles on demand. What we see here is politics in action. Each of the two men had their own jurisdiction but they were both quite happy to claim that it wasn't their problem when faced with a difficult case.

Herod was succeeded by his nephew, Agrippa I, who was not much better than his uncle. (Just to confuse matters, Agrippa I was sometimes also known as Herod. This is how he is referred to in the Acts of the Apostles, for example.) Agrippa had the Apostle James killed and Peter imprisoned.

However, we should not focus just on characters like Herod and Agrippa. We should also remember the fundamental role Judaism played in the creation of Christianity. Jesus was a good Jew who didn't come "to abolish the law and the prophets...but to fulfil them" (Mt 5:17). Unless we understand Judaism, we will never fully understand Christianity. We need the Old Testament as well as the New Testament if we are to understand why Jesus chose twelve Apostles, why he fasted in the desert for forty days, and why he drove the money changers out of the Temple, to give just a few examples.

When Christians were scattered throughout the Roman Empire, especially in the years after the destruction of the Temple in AD 70, they took the most fundamental Jewish beliefs with them. For example, the idea that there is just one God and that he is to be loved with our whole heart, mind, soul, and strength. This was a belief that Christians and Jews shared.

By contrast, most pagan Romans focused on their local gods, gods that were associated with their family or with the place where they lived. They didn't expect other people to join them in worshiping those same gods. The Christians were different. Like the Jews, they believed in one God and were prepared to die rather than compromise that belief by, for example, burning incense before a statue of the emperor. Unlike the Jews, they also believed that it was their task to spread the good news about God to the whole world.

The early Christians often worshiped in synagogues or in the Temple in Jerusalem if that was where they lived, but before long they realized that Christ's death and Resurrection meant that a different way of worshiping was not only possible but necessary. Saint Paul was a devout Jew before his conversion but he quickly came to understand that Christians no longer had to follow Jewish dietary laws, no longer had to worship in the Temple, and were no longer tied to the kingdom of Israel, but instead had an obligation to go out to the ends of the earth to preach the Gospel.

Christianity spread very quickly as Paul and others converted both Jews and gentiles. To teach and encourage these new converts, Paul traveled across the Roman Empire and also wrote letters to Christian communities in Rome, Greece (Corinth, Philippi, and Thessalonica), and what we now call Turkey (Ephesus, Galatia, and Colossae). Jerusalem was still a place where some of the first Christians worshiped, but it wasn't at the center of their religion as it was at the center of the Jews'. So, when Jerusalem fell to the Romans it didn't have as big an impact on Christianity as the Romans might have expected. Christianity had already spread far and wide and was more than capable of adapting to the new political situation.

The organization of the Church was crucial in enabling Christianity to survive and prosper. Because the Church had grown among the poor and powerless rather than among the political elite, it did not rely on the support of the state for its survival, so when the Roman emperors moved against it Christians were able to meet in secret and survive. The first Christians met in synagogues and homes rather than in churches and it was relatively straightforward for them to go underground when persecution started. Sometimes quite literally.

From Christian graffiti in the Roman catacombs (burial sites), we get a sense of Christians meeting in secret and communicating in code. The most famous example of a Christian code from this time was the fish or *ichthus* in Greek. For those in the know, these letters stood for Jesus Christ, Son of God, Savior.

Some Christians also used a letter code. Each letter of the Greek alphabet was given a separate number so Christians could write to each other without fear of having their letters intercepted. That is why some Christians signed off their letters with the number "99" instead of Amen. Unless you knew the code you would never be able to work out which word "99" referred to.

Christians further developed this code to create links between words like *Paul* and *wisdom*, *Easter* and *the good life*. In fact, it wasn't just Christians who did this; we've even got graffiti in Rome which through a similar number code links *Nero* with *killed his own mother* (which, in fact, he did).

However, there was more to the organization of the Church than the ability to go underground when persecution started. At the very heart of the new Church was the idea that authority was to be passed on from leader to leader, an idea known as apostolic succession. Even in those early days of Christianity there was a clear structure to the Church that enabled it to pass on the faith. As Saint Clement put it in his letter just a few years after the death of Jesus: "Now, the Gospel was given to the Apostles for us by the Lord Jesus Christ; and Jesus the Christ was sent by God. That is to say, Christ received his commission from God, and the Apostles theirs from Christ.... And as they went through the territories and townships preaching, they appointed their first converts—after testing them by the Spirit—to be bishops and deacons for the believers of the future." This meant that the Church could withstand even the most brutal of persecutions. For example, when Pope Sixtus II was beheaded in AD 258 along with several deacons, his job didn't die with him. When the persecution died down Dionysius was elected to succeed him as pope.

A third way that the Church was able to withstand persecution was by focusing on the afterlife. This was another way in which Christianity was fundamentally different from other religions in the Roman Empire. It focused on the hope of the world to come, which meant that martyrdom was to be welcomed if it came, though it wasn't to be sought out. The message of Jesus was pretty clear: the Christian's rewards were to come in the next world, not in this one.

Christianity did more than survive; it flourished under persecution. It was able to draw from the culture of the very people who were persecuting it. So much so that, in the end, it was the Roman Empire that collapsed, not the Church.

# CHAPTER 6

## *Saint Peter and the First Popes*

IN MANY WAYS IT IS A SURPRISE THAT ROME should have become the center of the Christian Church. Jerusalem was where Jesus's first disciples gathered to receive the Holy Spirit at Pentecost and it was in Jerusalem that Saint Peter, Saint James, and other Christian leaders lived and worked in the years after Jesus's death and Resurrection. However, there are several important reasons why the Christian center of gravity shifted to the capital of the Roman Empire. The key one was the martyrdom of the two great pillars of the Church, Saint Peter and Saint Paul, in Rome.

Saint Paul, unlike the rest of the Apostles, was a Roman citizen which gave him one distinct advantage: he was able to appeal to the emperor when arrested. This was a privilege he exercised to the full, as we can read in the Acts of the Apostles, where we find Paul writing while under house arrest in Rome. The Bible doesn't record what happened to him in Rome but it seems likely that he was executed there during Nero's persecution in about AD 64. According to Saint Clement, whose letter to the Corinthians we will discuss in more detail shortly, Saint Paul "was in bonds seven times, he was exiled, he was stoned. He preached in the East and in the West, winning a noble reputation for his faith. He taught righteousness to all the world; and after reaching the furthest limits of the West, and bearing testimony before kings and rulers, he passed out of this world and was received into the holy places. In him we have one of the greatest of all examples of endurance."

Saint Paul wasn't the only Christian leader to be martyred in Rome. Saint Peter, the undoubted leader of the early Church, also traveled to Rome and was executed there. Again we know very little about the details of his death but tradition has it that he was crucified upside down during the terrible persecution unleashed by the Emperor Nero. According to the Roman historian, Tacitus, Christians were executed in the gardens of Nero, which were outside the walls of Rome in the Vatican district. It may well have been that Saint Peter was executed next to the great obelisk that had been brought from Egypt by another terrible emperor, Caligula. 1500 years later this obelisk was moved into the great square in front of Saint Peter's where it can still be seen today. What had once been a symbol of the might of Rome now symbolizes the triumph of Roman Christianity over the Roman Empire.

If Saint Peter was executed by Nero it would have made sense for him to have been buried nearby, next to one of the roads out of the city, as was the custom of the time. According to the *Liber Pontificalis*, a record of the popes that was compiled over many years, "Peter entered the city of Rome when Nero was Caesar and there occupied the seat of the bishop for 25 years, 1 month and 8 days.... [H]e received the crown of martyrdom with Paul in the year 38 after the Lord's passion. He was buried also on the Via Aurelia, in the shrine of Apollo, near the place where he was crucified, near the palace of Nero, in the Vatican, near the triumphal district, on June 29."

That is why the first Christian emperor, Constantine, later built a great church in honor of Saint Peter in the Vatican district. The choice was deliberate; at the center of the church was the place where Saint Peter was buried. During excavations in the late 1930s and

1940s some bone fragments were found that may well have belonged to Saint Peter himself. What is certain is that the site where the bones were found was revered by the early Christians and that the early bishops of Rome were buried there rather than around the tomb of Saint Paul. Both men were revered but Saint Peter was the rock on which Christ built his Church.

Once Nero's persecution ended, the Christians of Rome drew great comfort from the fact that Peter and Paul, these two great Christian leaders, had met their end in their city. The tombs of the two Apostles became important centers of worship and the authority of the Apostles was passed on from one generation to the next. When Peter was killed, another man, called Linus, took his place as leader of the Church in Rome.

This was important because Christians from around the empire soon acknowledged the authority of the Church in Rome. One of the earliest indications of this authority comes in the First Epistle of Saint Clement I, which was probably written in about AD 96. Saint Clement was Bishop of Rome, after Linus, Cletus, and Peter himself. In his letter he tried to resolve problems that were troubling the Church in Corinth. What this shows is that his authority clearly stretched far beyond the boundaries of Rome. Not only did he believe that he had the right to write to a group of Christians in a distant city but he evidently expected them to take good note of what he was saying.

Saint Clement's letter is probably the earliest Christian document we possess with the exception of the New Testament itself, but it is not the only document to suggest the importance of Rome and Saint Peter. The most remarkable of these documents was written in extraordinary circumstances by Saint Ignatius of Antioch. Saint Ignatius, who was the third Bishop of

Antioch, was arrested during the reign of the Emperor Trajan somewhere between AD 98 and AD 117. He was then sent to Rome to be killed by wild beasts in the Flavian amphitheater. The reason we know about these events is that he sent seven letters to different Christian churches while he was on his way to Rome. In one of these letters to the Church in Rome, he describes traveling "by land and by sea, by night and by day, the whole way from Syria to Rome; chained as I am to ten savage leopards [in other words, a detachment of soldiers] who only grow more insolent the more gratuities they are given."

Chained to his guards, he was accompanied by local Christians from city to city and, far from fearing the martyrdom he was about to suffer, he welcomed it with open arms. In fact, one of the main reasons he wrote to the Romans was to beg them not to try to have him released. What is important for us in this chapter is some incidental information he gives us while writing about other matters. Firstly, he mentions the "chief place" that the Church in Rome holds. Secondly, he explains that he will not issue orders to the Roman Church "as though I were a Peter or a Paul." His authority differs from theirs. Where they led, he followed.

From an early date, the Bishop of Rome was regarded quite differently from bishops of other cities but it wasn't until much later that the Bishop of Rome became known as the pope. It also took many years before the Papacy itself (the role of the pope, if you like) developed into something close to what we would recognize today. It is very difficult to say exactly what powers the first popes had because not much evidence has survived, but it is clear that the Church very quickly became Roman after the destruction of the Temple in Jerusalem in AD 70.

So, who were these first popes? We don't have a great deal of information about them, but some intriguing facts have survived. The third pope, Cletus (also known as Anacletus), may have been a slave at some point of his life. Pope Callistus I (who was pope from AD 218 to 223) had an even more complicated background. Unfortunately, we only know about him through documents written by his enemies but it seems clear that he was originally a slave in Rome who was then sent to work as a slave laborer in the mines of Sardinia before being freed. Later, for reasons that have not come down to us, he became pope.

The early popes came from a number of different places, including Rome, Athens, and Africa (in the case of Victor I, who was pope from AD 189 to 199, and Miltiades, who reigned from 311 to 314). However, what really mattered was not their place of origin but their lives and deaths. Being pope was a risky business and most of the early popes were **martyred**.

It would be a mistake to think Christians were being hauled into the Colosseum and fed to the lions on a regular basis. (For a start, the Colosseum was only opened in AD 80, several years after Saint Peter and Saint Paul were martyred in Rome.)

However, as we have already seen, it is true that Christians and Jews were persecuted on a fairly regular basis, with the Jews (including Christian Jews) being expelled from Rome in AD 49 by the emperor Claudius, an event that is mentioned in passing in the Acts of the Apostles (chapter 18, verse 2). According to the Roman historian Suetonius, Claudius expelled the Jews because of "disturbances at the instigation of Chrestus." Suetonius was so unfamiliar with Christianity that he seems to have garbled his facts. "Chrestus" probably refers to Christ and the expulsion probably came about as a result of Christian-Jewish arguments getting out of hand in Rome's synagogues.

By AD 54 Jews were allowed back into Rome only for far worse persecution to start under the emperor Nero in AD 64. When a huge fire wiped out vast sections of Rome, Nero needed a scapegoat, especially when rumors began to spread that he had started the fire himself. He picked on the Christians. Many were killed, some in almost unimaginably horrible ways. However, far from wiping out the young religion, it actually seems to have strengthened it. In Tertullian's famous and powerful phrase, *etiam plures efficimur, quotiens metimur a vobis: semen est sanguis Christianorum*, which is often translated as, "The more we are mown down by you the more we grow: the blood of the martyrs is the seed of the Church," though, strictly speaking, a more accurate translation of the last part would be, "the blood of Christians is seed."

Christians were martyred throughout the first centuries of the Church's existence but there were several particularly intense periods of persecution: during the reigns of Nero (AD 54-68), Domitian (AD 81-96), Septimius Severus (AD 193-211), Decius (AD 249-251) and Diocletian (AD 284-305), with these last two waves of persecutions being particularly sustained.

We have already met Saint Ignatius of Antioch who was martyred during the reign of the emperor Trajan at the start of the second century. In his letter to the Christians in Rome he wrote that he wanted to die "for God" and prayed that they would "leave me to be a meal for the beasts, for it is they who can provide my way to God. I am His wheat, ground fine by the lions' teeth to be made purest bread for Christ." Saint Ignatius staked everything on being with God. That is what really mattered. As far as he was concerned, the whole earth would have been of no profit to him since "to die in Jesus Christ is better than to be monarch of earth's widest bounds." This tranquility in the face of death meant that he was ready to face terrible suffering because there was never any doubt about what was coming his way: "Fire, cross, beast-fighting, hacking and quartering, splintering of bone and mangling of limb, even the pulverizing of my entire body—let every horrid and diabolical torment come upon me, provided only that I can win my way to Jesus Christ!"

We have another account from later in the second century which, in many ways, is even more remarkable: a book called *The Martyrdom of Saints Perpetua and Felicitas*. Perpetua was about twenty-two years old and had recently had a baby when she was arrested in Carthage, a city in North Africa, during the reign of Septimius Severus. She was still a catechumen, which meant that she was receiving instruction in the Christian faith before being baptized. Her father was a pagan, so he put intense pressure on her after her arrest to deny her faith and to offer a sacrifice to the pagan gods for the emperor's health, which she steadfastly refused to do.

What is particularly interesting about this account is that parts of it seem to have been written by Perpetua herself while she was still alive. She described the darkness and stifling heat of the prison, and she wrote about the torment she felt at being separated from her baby "who was now faint from hunger." Eventually she "got permission for my baby to stay in prison with me, and at once I got better and was relieved from the distress and worry about my baby, and suddenly my prison became a palace, so that I preferred to be there rather than anywhere else."

We can sometimes feel cut off from the past, but moving passages like these remind us of what is unchanging throughout history. In the rest of the account, Perpetua describes visions she had in her prison cell as well as the huge psychological pressure she was put under by both her father and the governor, who had the power to have her killed or released. She tells us that she was still breastfeeding her son in prison but that he was taken away from her and given to her father. And then she writes that the governor "sentenced us all and he condemned us all to the beasts. We went down into the prison happy." What a remarkable sentence that is! After all the suffering she had gone through, she was still able to be happy because, as she wrote in another part of her account, "I cannot be anything except what I am, a Christian."

It is easy to focus on the gruesome details when looking at the deaths of the first Christian martyrs, but that isn't really the point. (In this case, Perpetua and Felicitas, her faithful slave, were killed in a rather unusual way: a mad cow was set loose and then, when that didn't finish them off, they were killed with a sword.) What really mattered was their resolute devotion to God and the amazing joy they demonstrated in the face of death.

Saint Ignatius, Saint Perpetua, and Saint Felicity are just a few of the many Christians who were killed in the first three centuries after the death of Christ. Despite this persecution, or maybe because of it, the Church grew and took advantage of the times when it was left in comparative peace.

Persecution came and went but we shouldn't ignore the fear factor: Christians could never be entirely sure of their safety until the mid-fourth century—Saint Justin Martyr, for example, was beheaded during the reign of a man who is often regarded as one of the good guys: the philosopher-emperor Marcus Aurelius. You might be safe under one emperor but you never knew what the attitude of the next emperor would be. What few Christians could have expected during the terrible years of Diocletian's reign in the fourth century was that Rome was about to get an emperor who was to do more than stop the persecution of the Christians: he was to become one.

# CHAPTER 7

# *The Emperor Constantine*

CHRISTIANS HAD A BAD TIME IN THE LATE third and early fourth centuries. The Emperor Diocletian (who reigned from AD 284 to AD 305) unleashed the fiercest persecutions the Church had ever known. Many Christians were killed and others, including some priests, gave up the faith to save themselves. But in AD 305 Diocletian retired from office and the Christians were able to take stock of their situation. They didn't know whether the persecutions would continue or get worse. What they couldn't have expected—what no one expected—was that the next emperor would convert from paganism to Christianity.

In order to explain what happened, we need to go back to Diocletian. Diocletian was a terrible persecutor of Christians but he was an astute politician. He realized that the Roman Empire had grown too large for any one man to control and so he created what was called the Tetrarchy, which means the rule of four people. Essentially what Diocletian did was divide the empire into two halves (the largely Greek-speaking East and the largely Latin-speaking West) and put one man (an augustus) in charge of each half, with an assistant (a caesar) to help him.

In theory, and sometimes in practice, this made it much easier to run the empire. The problem was that there were now four top jobs up for grabs and so more opportunities for rebellions if an army leader felt that he had missed out on one of the top jobs. This is what happened with Constantine. He expected to be appointed as caesar of the West and when he wasn't, he raised an army in Britain and marched on Gaul. After a lot more fighting he found himself just outside Rome ready to fight the Battle of the Milvian Bridge in AD 312 and here, on the eve of the battle, he had a life-changing experience.

There are two accounts of what happened next and we're not sure which one is the more accurate. According to the first account, an angel appeared to Constantine in a dream and ordered him to paint the *chi-rho* symbol on his soldiers' shields. These two Greek letters represent Christ, with *chi* being the equivalent of "ch" and *rho* being the Greek letter "r", the first letters in "Christ."

According to the second account, which appears in Eusebius's *History of the Church*, Constantine saw a cross in the sky and the words, "In this sign you will conquer" written on the sun.

Whichever account is closer to the truth, we know for certain that Constantine won the battle, became a Christian and became augustus of the West. In his whole career, he never lost a battle, but the really crucial one was the Battle of the Milvian Bridge. This was a must-win battle and he must have had doubts about the outcome. That is why his dream or vision was so important. That is why he took the completely unexpected step of becoming a Christian, of accepting the religion of what was still a small, minority group. Suddenly the Church and the Roman Empire were in uncharted territory. Christians were used to being tolerated at best and tortured and killed at worst but now, out of the blue, the emperor was a Christian too. So, what changed?

Firstly, Constantine (and Licinius, the augustus of the East who was still a pagan) issued what is usually called the Edict of Milan in AD 313. (In reality, it wasn't an edict and it wasn't issued from Milan, but the name stuck.)

This document granted Christians the toleration they had always been denied. Christianity was legal at last. But Constantine didn't stop there. He allowed bishops and other Christian officials to use the imperial post system, which was more of a free travel service than a way of posting letters. This meant they could visit their flocks and meet other bishops more easily. He also said that the Church didn't need to pay taxes to the state and started passing laws that fitted in with his Christian beliefs. Gladiatorial fights were banned, for instance, though the ban wasn't very well enforced at first. We will return to this in a later chapter.

Constantine also built churches. Two of the most famous Christian churches in Rome, Saint Peter's and Saint John Lateran, were built by Constantine at this time (though both have changed a great deal since then). We might take this for granted, but it was a huge change. Christianity had begun as an embattled religion. In order to survive, the first Christians had met secretly in people's homes or even in the catacombs (the burial grounds) under the streets of Rome. Now Christianity was able to become a public religion. Christians were now able to build churches. In fact, with a generous emperor on their side, they were able to worship in great churches that were built on some of the holiest sites in the empire.

Eventually Constantine fell out with Licinius and in AD 324 defeated him in battle just outside a place called Byzantium in what is modern-day Turkey. Constantine was now in charge of the whole Roman Empire and he wanted to keep it that way. Not one to shirk big decisions, he decided that Rome was too isolated. He wanted a new capital city that would be a central military and economic base from which to control the whole empire and he thought that Byzantium was just the place.

Now you may not have heard of Byzantium and that's because Constantine renamed it. He named it after himself. It became Constantinople. Now, I suppose it's entirely possible that you may not have heard of Constantinople either and that's because it was later renamed again, for reasons we won't go into now. This time it became Istanbul, and it's still the capital of Turkey today. And if you haven't heard of Istanbul, you'll have to have a word with your Geography teacher.

So, by the time Constantine died in AD 337, having ruled for longer than anyone other than Augustus, the Roman Empire was a very different place from what it had been when he came to power in AD 312. The emperor was in total control. The empire had a new capital. And Christianity, though not yet the empire's official religion, was legal. In fact, by the time of Constantine's death perhaps fifty percent of the empire's citizens were Christians. Such rapid growth is quite remarkable and helps explain why the bad old days of widespread persecution didn't return after Constantine's death. With the exception of the Emperor Julian (AD 360–363) all the emperors who followed Constantine were Christians, at least in name. Wealthy Romans gave money to the Church. Churches were built. Christians no longer feared for their lives.

It was a mixed blessing of course. Constantine was keen to protect the Church but he also thought he had the right to influence it. That was often a problem, though sometimes the Church was grateful for his support. Never more so than when he called the Council of Nicaea in AD 325.

Each week in church we say the Nicene **Creed**, a statement of the Church's most important beliefs. However, we don't often think about where the Nicene

Creed came from. At the center of Christianity is revelation, but not the revelation of a book or even of a set
of doctrines, but of a person. At the heart of Christianity is Christ. Jesus taught his disciples but his message
wasn't simply conveyed in words. At least as important were his actions: his miracles and, above all, his
death and Resurrection. So, after the Ascension, after
Jesus returned to his Father, the Apostles had a lot of
thinking to do. With the help of the Holy Spirit, they
had to work out the significance of what they had seen
and experienced.

It was Saint Thomas who first called Jesus "my Lord
and my God" (Jn 20:28), but even after Saint Thomas
and the first Christians realized that it was God himself who had come to earth and lived with them, they
still had a lot of working out to do. A lot of this early
theological thinking can be seen in Saint Paul's letters
and other parts of the New Testament but the Church's
work didn't stop there. If Jesus was God then how
exactly was he related to the Father? In what way was
he both God and man?

Eventually the Church developed the complex doctrine of the Trinity to explain what had already been
revealed in the person of Christ and the work of the
Holy Spirit in making the Father known in the Church,
but there were many arguments along the way. Different thinkers came up with different ideas about who
Christ was and some of them, to put it simply, got it
wrong. These inaccurate ideas about God are known as
heresies and one of the most persistent and troublesome of these heresies was Arianism.

Arius (AD 256–336) was a priest from Alexandria
and he taught that Jesus was not equal to God the
Father. Instead, according to Arius, he was created by
the Father and was a sort of halfway house between

God and man. Some of the statements we make in the Nicene Creed today were first written in response to the Arian heresy. By affirming that Christ was "God from God, Light from Light, True God from True God, begotten not made" and "consubstantial with the father," the Church was teaching that Jesus Christ was perfect God and perfect man, not a semi-divine being as Arius taught.

When Constantine converted to Christianity, Arius's ideas (Arian ideas, in other words) were causing great problems within the Church. Many Christians were taken in by this heresy and divisions occurred across the Christian world, especially in North Africa, where Arius and his greatest opponent, Saint Athanasius, lived. Constantine's answer was to call a general council of the Church. Now that Christianity had the emperor's backing, bishops were able to travel from all over the Christian world to meet and resolve difficulties, just as the Apostles and Saint Paul had done when they met in Jerusalem. On this occasion, the bishops met at a place called Nicaea near Constantinople in AD 325 to resolve the questions that Arius had raised about the divinity of Christ. Nicaea was centrally located, which meant there was a greater chance that Constantine would be able to get bishops from both the east and the west to attend.

The council of Nicaea was the first of twenty-one general (otherwise known as ecumenical) councils that met to deal with problems that affected the whole Church. The general councils that met during the period covered in this book were the first council of Nicaea (AD 325), the first council of Constantinople (AD 381), the council of Ephesus (AD 431), the council of Chalcedon (AD 451), the second council of Constantinople (AD 553), the third council of Constantinople (AD 680–681), the second council of Nicaea (AD 787), and the fourth council of Constantinople (AD 869).

The first council of Nicaea ruled decisively against Arius and drew up the Nicene Creed to help Christians understand their faith. This creed was a hugely important statement of belief. Pagan religions didn't go in for statements of belief. Truth wasn't an important concept for pagans, but Christianity was different. Christianity wasn't just another way of thinking about life. It wasn't a set of religious practices that some people enjoyed on a Sunday. Christianity claimed to be true.

In fact, Christianity had Christ at the center and Christ said: "I am the way, and the truth, and the life" (Jn 14:6). Christians couldn't be free and easy about what they taught. If God had revealed himself to man then doctrine mattered. And if doctrine mattered, then Christians needed to know the truth and to be protected from false teaching. That is why Christians learned the Nicene Creed. That is why schoolchildren in sixth-century Egypt practiced copying the Nicene Creed onto shards of pots as handwriting practice. That is why we still recite the Nicene Creed today.

However, simply creating the Nicene Creed did not end the problems caused by Arian ideas. Arius and his supporters grew in confidence, partly because they won the support of some of Constantine's sons and partly because they were incredibly successful missionaries. A Gothic Arian priest called Wulfilas converted many of the so-called barbarian tribes we will meet in a later chapter and even Constantine himself seems to have drifted into Arian beliefs.

If it wasn't obvious already, it now became very clear that the Church could not rely on emperors to maintain correct beliefs or doctrines. Constantine's successors as emperors continued to take an active interest in the Church, calling councils of bishops when further theological problems arose, but the Church was quite clear about who made the final decisions: it had to be the bishops themselves—often known as the council fathers—chief among whom was the Bishop of Rome. In fact, it was the Bishop of Rome who decided whether the council was simply a local council dealing with local problems or an ecumenical council with the power to **legislate** for the whole Church. As the Catechism of the Catholic Church puts it: "'The college of bishops exercises power over the universal Church in a solemn manner in an ecumenical council.' But 'there never is an ecumenical council which is not confirmed or at least recognized as such by Peter's successor.'"

This didn't stop emperors calling councils and it didn't stop these councils doing good work but it did mean that the decision-making powers of these councils never belonged to the emperors. Emperors may have been the most powerful men on earth but the Church made sure there were clear limits to their powers.

# CHAPTER 8

## *Relics*

IT WASN'T JUST POPES AND EMPERORS WHO changed the world. A remarkable woman called Helena also did her bit. Helena was the Emperor Constantine's mother and when she was about eighty years old she set off on a remarkable pilgrimage to Jerusalem. Before Constantine became emperor and while Christianity was seen as a danger to the Roman Empire, Christians had few opportunities to make a pilgrimage to the holy sites and even fewer opportunities to carry out archaeological work when they got there. But that was what Helena intended to do. She wanted to find the Cross on which Jesus had been crucified and that is what she did. Helped by Saint Macarius, bishop of the city, she eventually managed to uncover three crosses, one of which was identified as the True Cross.

Why did she think such a quest important? Why did she want to find the Cross? Why did Christians want to have what she discovered? In order to answer those questions we need to think about the nature of Christianity itself.

Christianity is a very physical religion. The **Incarnation**, Crucifixion, and Resurrection are all physical events. The **sacraments** are based upon the simple but profound idea that we get to the spiritual through the physical. Christianity is not essentially a religion of ideas but a religion that is centered on water, bread, and wine. (Of course, ideas matter too. They matter enormously. But the physical facts come first and the ideas follow after.)

So, it's perhaps no surprise that the physical remains of the saints, and items associated with them, became important to the Church. These remains are known as relics, which means "left behind"; they are what the saints left behind when they entered heaven. The reason they are important is because they help us move from the earthbound to the heavenly.

To understand why they thought this, we need a little theology. Christians don't merely follow a set of ideas, or a set of rules about moral and religious life. At the heart of Christianity is a person, Jesus Christ, perfect God and perfect man, and because God became man, what was just human could now be a path to God. It was because God himself worked, ate, got tired, and lived a fully human life that Helena went in search of the True Cross. Because God had lived on earth in real places and died in a real place, those places became hugely important.

But we need to go a step further. It's not just places that became charged with the grandeur of God but people too. Since God became Man "for us men and for salvation," being a Christian brings us into a life of close communion with others. Saint Paul describes us all as members of Christ's Mystical Body, with Christ as its Head. All of us. The living and the dead. The ties that unite Christians are not broken by death. This is why the veneration of relics became so important to the early Christians; they were a very powerful reminder of the communion of saints.

According to Saint Basil (who lived between AD 330 and 379), "those who touch the bones of the martyrs participate in their sanctity." Saint Gregory of Nazianzus explained how this worked by writing that the "bodies of the martyrs have the same power as their holy souls, whether one touches them or just venerates them. Just a few drops of their blood, the signs of their sufferings, can effect the same as their bodies." That is why the followers of Saint Polycarp, Bishop of Smyrna, who was martyred in c. AD 156, "took up his bones, which are more valuable than precious stones and finer than refined gold, and deposited them in a suitable place. There gathering together, as we are able, with joy and gladness, the Lord will permit us to celebrate the birthday of his martyrdom in commemoration of those who have already fought in the contest." By the end of the fourth century, gathering at martyrs' tombs on the anniversary of their martyrdom was common practice. After a strict fast and an all-night, candlelit vigil, there would be Mass at the tomb and a procession with the martyrs' relics.

In the ancient world bodies were buried outside the city walls either in catacombs, some of which can still be visited today, or in monumental tombs that lined streets such as the Via Appia, one of the main roads out of Rome. It was in places like these that the first Christians gathered and in places like these that the first churches were built, above the graves of great saints like Saint Peter.

After a while the Christians started to dig up some of these martyrs' bodies—in a way that appalled Jews, Greeks, and Romans—either to move them to a new location (a new church, for example) or in order to divide them up so that different parts of the saint's remains could be taken to different places for veneration. Before long relics were being placed in altars. In fact, the Seventh Ecumenical Council of Nicaea in AD 787 decreed that "in venerable churches consecrated without relics of the holy martyrs, the installation of relics should take place along with the usual prayers. And if in future any bishop is found out consecrating a church without relics, let him be deposed as someone who has flouted the ecclesiastical traditions." To this day fixed altars in Catholic churches must contain a relic. That is why the priest always kisses the altar at the start of Mass. He is doing homage to the saint or saints whose relics are under the altar stone.

Digging up graves of the saints led to two further developments. Firstly, some bodies were found uncorrupted. When Saint Hilarion was dug up so that his remains could be moved, it was discovered that "his whole body remained perfect, as if he were still alive, giving off such a fragrance that you would think it had been anointed with perfumed oils," as Saint Jerome put it. The lack of corruption was an important indication of the dead person's sanctity. Secondly the range of relics was greatly extended. In addition to visiting the tombs of the martyrs and collecting their bones, Christians also started to collect individual body parts, fragments of clothing, and even objects that had been in contact with the saints. The most important of these objects was the wood of the Cross since it was on the Cross that Jesus had won his great victory over death. That is why Saint Helena went on a pilgrimage to Jerusalem in AD 326 and that is why we remember her today.

# CHAPTER 9

## *Books and The Book*

WE TAKE THE EXISTENCE OF THE BIBLE FOR granted but we rarely ask why certain books rather than others became part of the Old or New Testaments. In fact, there has been quite a lot of discussion within both Judaism and Christianity about which books should be accepted as part of Scripture, as part of the "canon" as it is called.

Even today there are differences of opinion. Protestants don't accept certain books from the Catholic Old Testament in their version of the Bible and the Coptic Church in Egypt includes two letters of Saint Clement in its canon. The number of books in the Bible ranges from eighty-one in the Ethiopian Orthodox version to sixty-six in Protestant versions.

So how were decisions made and which books didn't make the cut?

The first point to remember, as we have already seen, is that Christianity is a religion that is centered on a person, not a book. The Word of God, as Saint John's Gospel tells us, is Jesus Christ, the eternal Son of the Father, made man. The books of the New Testament came later. Some of the first Christians died before the New Testament was written but that doesn't mean they missed out. Far from it. The Apostles preached and taught and some of this living Tradition was later written down by the Gospel writers and others.

The Church had to decide which of these later books and letters were divinely inspired. This was not necessarily an easy task because a lot of written material was passed around the early Christian communities, including gospels, letters, and **apocalyptic** writings. Some of these books were divinely inspired and so ended up in the Bible, some are interesting (and even instructive) but not part of Scripture, and some are just plain wacky. In the *Infancy Gospel of Thomas*, for example, Jesus not only brings clay birds to life but he also kills two children who annoy him. It's no surprise that this book didn't make it into the Bible!

So how did the Church decide? How can anyone decide which books should be in the Holy Book? Christians are not like Muslims; they don't believe that their Book was dictated by an angel. The Bible is the word of God but it is also the word of man. The key issue for the Church, therefore, was apostolicity; to make it into the Bible, writings had to come directly or indirectly from the Apostles because they were the ones who were with Jesus "all the time...beginning from the baptism of John until the day when he was taken up" (Acts 1:21–22).

The first person to complete a fixed list of New Testament writings was a second-century heretic called Marcion. He rejected the God of the Old Testament and created his own version of the New Testament with just a single gospel made up of stories from different gospels. This rejection of the Church's Jewish past was a terrible mistake and so the Church responded quickly to Marcion's heretical challenge. It realized that it had to fix the canon of Scripture and it had to get it right.

This process took many years. The first document that refers to the twenty-seven books of the New Testament we now accept is the Easter letter of Saint Athanasius in 367 but more important was the decision of Pope Damasus around the year 380 to commission a new translation of the Bible into Latin. This translation, which became known as the Vulgate, was carried out by one of the more remarkable characters from the early Church: Saint Jerome. Saint Jerome was so keen to do a good job, to discern the word of God, that he lived for a while in a cave next to the Cave of the Nativity, where Jesus, the Word made Flesh, had been born. This was God's work; not his.

However, not even the Vulgate was the finished version. It wasn't until the Council of Trent in the sixteenth century that the Church definitively stated which books were divinely inspired and, even after that, questions were raised (about the end of Saint Mark's Gospel, for example). Catholics had to wait until the First Vatican Council in the nineteenth century to get the Church's official ruling on those passages. In other words, the reason we have the Bible as we have it today is because of the Church. The Church, inspired by the Holy Spirit, tells us which books should be included in the Bible.

But all this discussion about the Christians' holy book raises another basic question: what is a book?

For the Greeks, Romans, and the Jews of Jesus's day, the word "book" actually meant a "roll" or "scroll." Think of the time when Jesus was asked to read in the synagogue. He took the scroll, unrolled it until he came to the passage that referred to the coming of the Messiah, and then handed it back and sat down. He didn't flick through the pages of anything we would recognize as a book.

However, all that was to change with the invention of the *codex*, a collection of sheets (of either papyrus or parchment) that were folded into pages and then bound together in what were called quires. At first these new books became fashionable as miniature presents but the reason they caught on was that Christians used them for their Bible. As one historian put it: "The classics followed where the Gospels led."

We're not quite sure why Christians favored the *codex* or *codices*. Maybe it was because they were smaller than scrolls and so could be hidden more easily during times of persecution. Maybe it was because the whole Bible could be fitted between two covers rather than requiring lots of separate scrolls. Maybe Christians were simply trying to distinguish themselves from the pagans and the Jews who still used scrolls. Whatever the reason, the book was here to stay.

Very few books remain from this time, which means that we can very easily forget how many books there were in existence. The great library of Alexandria alone contained something like 500,000 rolls and so scholars from around the world came to Egypt to study there. Unfortunately parts of the library were destroyed by conflict. When Julius Caesar besieged the city in 48 BC, for example, the fire he started to destroy the Egyptian fleet spread to storehouses near the harbor, destroying something like 40,000 rolls in the process.

However, books could be found throughout the ancient world, not just in Alexandria; Pliny the Elder, for instance, claimed that he read 2,000 volumes when doing the research for his book on *Natural History*. There were great libraries, including personal libraries, across the ancient world and cities also had their own archives where they stored thousands of documents. Virtually none of these have survived.

This means that we no longer have important books by some of the greatest writers of the Greek, Roman, and early Christian worlds. Some disintegrated over time, some were destroyed in war, and some were lost for quite different reasons. When the nineteenth-century biblical scholar Constantin von Tischendorf went to Saint Catherine's Monastery in the Sinai desert in search of old books, he found sections

of the oldest known edition of the Bible being torn up
as paper for the fire. The monastery was cold and the
monks thought that it was quite a good idea to use old
bits of paper to keep themselves warm.

Even more intriguing is a letter from Peter the Venerable, abbot of the great French monastery of Cluny, to
the monks of the Grande Chartreuse with this request:
"And please send us the larger volume of the holy father
Augustine which almost at the beginning contains his
letters to Saint Jerome, and those of Saint Jerome to
him. For a large part of ours when it was in one of our
obediences was accidentally eaten by a bear." There
must be a great story behind that little detail; unfortunately, we don't know what it is!

We know a great deal about the ancient world but we
should never forget just how much we have lost. Tens
of thousands of pieces of evidence have disappeared
over time, simply because paper and papyrus are so
fragile. Nonetheless, some ancient books have been
preserved, often in very surprising ways. There is a
wall in Turkey on which you can read a philosophical
treatise by Diogenes of Oenoanda, for example. When
it was complete it had 25,000 words and spread over
nearly 2800 square feet. Other unusual survivals are
the books that were stored in houses at Herculaneum
when hot liquid mud from Mount Vesuvius poured over
them in AD 79. Some of these rolls were carbonized,
which means that they can just about be unrolled, separated, and read by very careful archaeologists. Unfortunately, the early archaeologists were not always that
careful; some of the books were damaged beyond
repair because the first archaeologists to work in the
city thought they were simply lumps of coal.

Another way of preserving papyrus, as we shall see
in a later chapter, is to keep it in absolutely bone dry

conditions. In the Egyptian desert, for example. The oldest papyrus roll that has been found so far is about 5,000 years old and was discovered in an Egyptian tomb. Imagine the excitement as the archaeologists unrolled it to find out what had been written by those early Egyptians. Imagine their disappointment when they discovered that it was completely blank; almost certainly it had been left that way so the dead man could use it in the afterlife. Sometimes we have to accept that there are gaps in our knowledge, leaving us to do what we can with the evidence that remains.

# CHAPTER 10

## Herculaneum, Pompeii, and Everyday Life

WHEN WE LOOK BACK ALMOST TWO THOUsand years, it can be very difficult to get a sense of how ordinary people lived. Part of the problem, of course, is that there are no ordinary people. Different people in different parts of the empire had quite different experiences. The life of an educated man in Rome was quite different from that of a female slave in Britain. Nonetheless, we can get some idea of everyday life through archaeology, and what we have at Herculaneum and Pompeii are among the most remarkable archaeological sites in the world.

The story is well known: Mount Vesuvius erupted in August AD 79, destroying the city of Pompeii and simultaneously preserving a snapshot of Roman life for later generations to discover. Or so we have been told.

However, the picture is not quite as simple as that. For a start, we need to remember that it wasn't simply Pompeii that was destroyed. In some ways, the destruction of Herculaneum was more important in historical terms. Pompeii was covered by a terrible volcanic ash but Herculaneum was wiped out by a **pyroclastic** surge that reached 752 degrees Fahrenheit. This meant that any organic material in the city—including wood, leather, and food—was **carbonized** before being buried under thirty feet of volcanic rock. Nowhere else in the world will you find libraries of carbonized papyrus, carbonized loaves with the baker's stamp still clearly visible, carbonized figs prepared for the table, and even, saddest of all, a baby's crib—carbonized.

There is a great deal we still don't know, partly because a quarter of Pompeii and over half of Herculaneum hasn't yet been excavated. Some of our unanswered questions are very basic. We're not even sure, for example, when Vesuvius erupted. Pliny the Younger gives the dates as 24th–25th August and he was an eyewitness, but there are reasons for thinking that his date may be wrong if only because his letters were later copied and different copies given different dates.

August may have been the date he originally gave, but we know that he only wrote about the eruption twenty-five years after the event. We also know that archaeologists have found portable heaters that had been used on the day of the explosion and a whole lot of autumnal fruits, which suggests that there's a problem with the dating, especially when we discover that a lot of the people fleeing the city seem to have been wearing heavy woolen clothes. If you've been to Italy during the summer you'll know that you don't need the heating on and that heavy woolen clothes are not the ideal choice of clothing for August. Perhaps the volcano erupted later in the year than historians previously thought.

The final piece of evidence that Pliny got the date wrong has only recently been discovered. A short piece of writing in charcoal has been found on the side of a building. In all likelihood, it was written by a worker renovating a house. It gives the date as 17th October, almost two months after Pompeii was destroyed according to Pliny. Again the evidence suggests that Pliny got his date wrong and that Vesuvius actually erupted in late October.

There are other basic questions that we don't have answers to, like how many people lived in and around Pompeii. An educated guess puts the number at 12,000 in the city and 24,000 in the surrounding area, but it is only an estimate. Sometimes the main thing to emerge from a great historical discovery is a reminder of just how little we know about the past.

Nonetheless, even with all these provisos, it is possible to discover a great deal about life in Pompeii and Herculaneum in AD 79. For example, who would have guessed that Pompeii had a one-way system in operation—we can tell this from bollards in the roads and the ruts made on the surface by cartwheels—or that people were killed burrowing back *into* Pompeii?

Pompeii was a rich city and the temptation to strip houses of their valuables (even if it meant risking your life to get back in) was too great for some people. Archaeologists have discovered the words "House tunneled" scratched by the main door of one house in the city, presumably as a message to the rest of the looters, and in another house the remains of two adults and a child have been found along with a pickaxe and hoe. Some historians have argued that they were killed when the tunnel they were digging into the house collapsed on top of them.

And what about the graffiti? There are all sorts of marks on the walls. On one patch we can see "Epaphroditus cum Thalia hac" which simply means "Epaphroditus and Thalia were here" but before we start thinking that the Pompeians were just like us, we need to look further along the same patch of wall to see a quotation from the poet Lucretius: "suabe mari magno." In case you're wondering, that means "How sweet it is on the mighty sea." I've not seen any graffiti like that near where I live.

There is a lot of graffiti in Pompeii but it needs to be treated with the same care as any other historical sources. Take these comments about a famous gladiator from the time, for example: "Celadus, heartthrob of the girls" and "Celadus, the girls' idol." Does this graffiti tells us about Celadus's popularity? Not at all, because the writing was found inside the gladiatorial barracks. In other words, it was almost certainly written by one of the gladiators, probably Celadus himself. Where the words were written suggests who they were written by, which in turn suggest how reliable—or unreliable—they are.

One of the problems with Herculaneum and Pompeii is that we have almost too many artifacts. We can easily assume that no interpretation is needed, that what the remains tell us is obvious. The truth of the matter is that we still need to think and we still need to ask questions.

So let's start with a simple one. What can we see in Pompeii? Obviously, we can see remains of a Roman city, but what sort of remains? The remains of a city that was severely damaged by an earthquake in AD 63 (or maybe AD 62), that was destroyed by the eruption of Vesuvius in AD 79, that has been plundered (in different ways) by thieves and archaeologists, and that has deteriorated since being exposed to the elements in the twentieth century. In fact, what we see today is the result of a whole host of historical events, not just the explosion of Vesuvius. The picture is complicated by the fact that Vesuvius exploded again (though not so dramatically) in 1944 and that a terrible earthquake in 1980 caused great destruction. In other words, what we see today is not what survived the eruption of Vesuvius in AD 79 but what has survived volcanic eruptions, earthquakes, the action of the weather, visitors, thieves, and archaeologists over the last 2000 years. Not to mention the many reconstructions, some of which are more accurate than others. If you want to see what survived the eruption you can visit the remains of the city but you also have to visit museums where the most valuable objects are stored.

It's also important to remember that what we see in Pompeii and Herculaneum today is not a snapshot of everyday life. The Romans were not stupid. When Vesuvius started to spew ash and molten rock, they didn't simply sit around and wait to be killed. Something like two thirds of Pompeii's population seems to have fled before the worst of the explosion took place. Why did the others not leave with them? Perhaps they were too old or infirm. Perhaps they wanted to protect their property. It's impossible to say for sure. What is clear is that we've still got a lot of work to do if we're to make sense of all the many wonderful remains that have been found.

If we are trying to come to grips with everyday life in the Roman Empire, we have to think and analyze carefully. For our final example, let's have a think about the food that was eaten in Pompeii. One place to start is with an interesting list written on the atrium wall of a house. A list of different foods and a few other objects, with their prices, divided into eight days. It may be a shopping list.

Unfortunately, there are various problems with interpreting the list. The first is that we are not absolutely sure what some of the Latin words mean. Was a "sittule" a bucket? Was an "inltynium" a type of lamp? What exactly were "hxeres"? Even when we know what the words mean, we are not always sure what the products were. The list refers to "bread," "coarse bread," and "bread for the slave," but we don't really know the difference between each of these loaves.

Even with all these lacunae (or gaps) in our knowledge, we can try to draw some conclusions about everyday life. It seems that bread was a really important part of the diet, as were oil and wine, but there were other purchases too, including sausage, cheese, onions, leeks, and whitebait. Similar lists elsewhere in Pompeii include pork, cabbage, beetroot, mustard, mint, and salt. Sometimes these hints are backed up by other evidence, such as the tombstone of a former slave called Nigella which describes her as a public pig-keeper. More significant is a vineyard just north of Pompeii which has been carefully excavated. Tiny traces of seed and pollen have been analyzed, which have revealed that more than eighty different plants were grown there, including olives, apricots, peaches, almonds, and figs. What we don't know is who bought these goods.

Maybe this is the main lesson that Pompeii and Herculaneum have to teach us: that historians have to be humble. There is so much they do not know and never will know. Or to put it another way, we began this chapter in search of everyday life and discovered that it was an impossible task, though maybe we learned something along the way.

# CHAPTER 11

## Rome, Roman Britain, and a Few Places In Between

NOW THAT WE HAVE GOT OUT OF THE CITY of Rome we need to keep traveling. Let's go to Roman Britain. In fact, let's work out how Romans would have traveled from Rome to Britain.

Stanford University has done some wonderful work in producing an interactive map that allows us to examine how long an average journey would take to places in the empire in about AD 200. It is based on all sorts of interesting historical data which we won't go into now. Instead we are going to look at how long it might take to get from Rome to Londinium (which you will not be surprised to hear is what London was called at the time).

It all depended on when you were traveling and what form of transport you used. A rapid military march in July, for example, might take 23.7 days on average. In January the army would have taken an extra five days to get to London.

However, it was (just about) possible to do the journey even quicker than that. If you relied on horse relay, hiring a fresh horse every twenty-four hours, you could get from Rome to London in a mere 9.2 days in July. This option would have been extremely expensive.

Neither of these examples is particularly realistic though. It is highly unlikely that anyone would have needed to get from Italy to Britain in that much of a hurry and if a revolt needed to be crushed the army would more probably have come from Gaul than from Rome. Much more likely was the journey from London to Rome by merchants wanting to sell goods. For people like this what mattered was price, how cheaply they could transport their goods. And the cheapest way to make the journey would have taken something like 53.6 days, almost eight weeks.

What does all this tell us? A great deal and yet not very much. The first point to make is that long-distance travel was certainly possible. We tend to assume that people in the distant past stuck to their own villages and, for many citizens of the Roman Empire, this would have been the case. However, it is also true that one consequence of the *pax Romana*, the peace the Roman Empire imposed upon the Western world, was that many people were able to travel many hundreds of miles from their birthplaces.

It is also worth asking which routes were taken, so let's compare the quickest and the slowest options. Which route would a Roman have taken to get from Rome to London if he wanted to get there as quickly as possible and which route would a merchant have taken to get from London to the markets of Rome as cheaply as possible?

The first and fastest route would have been along the western Italian coast through Cosa and Pisae (Pisa) to Luna (Luni), where a boat would have been taken to Genua (Genoa). By the end of day three our imaginary Roman would have reached Forum Iulii (Frejus). By the end of day four he would have got to Arelate (Arles). He would then have traveled up through Gaul, passing through Vienna (Vienne), Lugdunum (Lyon), Augustodunum (Autun), and Durocortorum (Reims) until he reached Gesoriacum (Boulogne), where he would have taken a ship either to Rutupiae (Richborough in Kent) or directly to Londinium itself. The total distance would have been 1293 miles.

If, by contrast, a merchant wanted to travel cheaply from London to Rome he would have traveled entirely by sea, sailing along the English Channel, along the coasts of what we now call France and Spain and then into the Mediterranean, stopping to take on supplies at Rutupiae, Durnovaria (Dorchester), Civitas Namnetum (Nantes), Portus Blendium (Santander), Flavium Brigantium (Betanzos), Olisipo (Lisbon), Gades (Cadiz), and Caralis (Cagliari) before eventually docking at Ostia. The total distance would have been 3402 miles.

So, what does all this tell us? It reminds us of the importance of shipping routes for the Romans and the Greeks. The Romans were not just great road builders; they used rivers and the sea as transport routes too. As Socrates put it, "We live round the sea like ants and frogs round a pond." The Roman Empire was not simply European; it was built around the Mediterranean (or *Mare Nostrum* —Our Sea—as the Romans called it). Control of every side of the Mediterranean was vital for the Romans and the loss of North Africa, when it eventually happened, was devastating. Rome (and Italy more widely) relied on grain imports from around the empire but especially from North Africa (which might surprise us today).

The Roman world was both bigger and smaller than we are sometimes led to think. It was bigger than Europe but small enough to travel around quickly. And from AD 43 onward it was big enough to include many (but not all) parts of Britain. The emperor Claudius succeeded in gaining control where Julius Caesar had failed but we might wonder why he bothered with Britain at all. The Romans all agreed that Britain was at the very ends of the earth. What's more, the British, the Scots, and the Picts caused the Romans a lot of trouble over the years. So why did they bother invading?

The Romans wanted Britain partly so they could keep their troublesome neighbors under control, partly because they wanted the prestige that came from conquering the far ends of the earth, and partly for the material resources. Britain had tin and other resources that the Romans needed for their vast empire. But we need more detail than this. So it's high time we had a proper look at Roman Britain and in particular at a place called Verulamium.

When the Romans conquered part of Britain in AD 43 they came across a settlement called Verlamion. Renaming the place Verulamium, the Romans did what they always did in these situations: they rebuilt the place to look like pretty much any Roman town in any part of their extensive empire. A forum was constructed and a large bath house was built.

But before we start getting carried away with the idea that Roman civilization replaced British barbarity, we need to look at what was there before the Romans arrived. The surprising reality was that Verlamion wasn't doing too badly for itself. Archaeologists have found that even before the Romans arrived, the people of Verlamion were importing grapes, figs and wine from Italy. Their diet seems to have been good, they were minting gold, silver, and bronze coins, they were getting tableware from Gaul and ivory from much further afield. Theirs was not a primitive society.

However, when Queen Boudicca led the Iceni in their rebellion against the Romans in AD 60, she decided to destroy not just Camulodunum (Colchester) and Londinium (London) but Verulamium as well. As the Roman historian Tacitus put it: "Ruin fell on the town of Verulamium, for the barbarians, who delighted in plunder and were indifferent to all else, passed by the fortresses with military garrisons, and attacked whatever offered most wealth to the spoiler, and was unsafe for defense."

After Boudicca's rebellion was crushed, the Romans rebuilt Verulamium in spectacular fashion. As well as an enormous forum and massive public baths, they built a basilica that was over 328 feet long, at least nine temples, and many private houses. A theater that could seat several thousand people was added at a later date. Archaeologists have also discovered evidence of simple daily life: items such as tweezers, nail cleaners, and ear scoops; knives and spoons in a folding set; dice and game boards; broaches, necklaces, and hairpins.

But none of this explains why we remember Verulamium today. We remember the place because of an obscure soldier who lived in the town. We remember Verulamium because of a man called Alban.

According to Saint Gildas (a Welsh monk) and Saint Bede (an English monk) who have passed on most of what we know about the early history of Britain, Alban was a soldier who sheltered a Christian priest who was trying to escape persecution. He was so impressed by the man's piety that he became a Christian himself but was captured and executed after failing to offer public sacrifices to the gods. He was, in other words, the first British martyr.

Bede tells us that "Saint Alban suffered on the twenty-second day of June near the city of Verulamium, which the English now call Verlamacaestir or Vaeclingacaestir. Here, when the peace of Christian times was restored, a beautiful church worthy of his martyrdom was built, where sick folk are healed and frequent miracles take place to this day."

However, we no longer call the town Verlamion, Verulamium, Verlamacaestir or Vaeclingacaestir. We call it Saint Albans.

# CHAPTER 12

## India, China, Iraq, Ethiopia, and a Few Places In Between

TRAVEL DID NOT SIMPLY HAPPEN FROM EAST to West. There were plenty of trade routes that took merchants in the opposite direction, including the famous Silk Roads (as they were later called) that ran between Europe and China. Silks, spices, and many other goods were transported across vast distances in the ancient world, so it is hardly surprising that ideas spread too.

The Christian message spread in different ways. Sometimes, it was passed on by merchants and other travelers. You might remember the story in the Acts of the Apostles about Saint Philip meeting an Ethiopian on his way home, for example. It is likely that he evangelized some of the country on his return. However, we know a great deal more about events in the early fourth century when a philosopher from Tyre in modern-day Lebanon was killed on the East coast of Africa while on his way to India with two young relatives. These young boys, whose names were Aedesius and Frumentius, were taken to the king where they became his cup-bearer and his treasurer respectively. Frumentius became particularly influential and soon gathered Christians from among the Roman merchants in the city and set up a place for them to worship. Eventually he traveled to Alexandria, where the great Athanasius was bishop, and begged for a bishop to be appointed to strengthen the faith of the people. Athanasius and his council of priests responded by appointing Frumentius himself as the first Bishop of Axum. Soon afterward Ezana, the Emperor of the Aksumite kingdom (which later became known as Ethiopia) converted to Christianity and established it as the state religion. The Ethiopian Church was established very early in the history of Christianity and has some of the most amazing churches on the planet, since they were carved directly out of the rock. They are quite unlike any other buildings you are ever likely to see.

Christianity also spread through networks of Jewish communities, which were already to be found in the Persian Empire as well as in the Roman Empire. In some instances it also spread as a result of persecution. When the Church was attacked, Christians sometimes fled and were sometimes deported, taking the Christian message with them. A prime example of this can be seen in the third century when large numbers of Christians were deported from Persia. One of these exiles was Demetrius, the Bishop of Antioch, who simply moved onto a place called Beth Lapat (which is today called Gundeshapur in Iran). He set up a new bishopric there and the Church continued to grow. Before long cities such as Merv (in modern-day Turkmenistan) and Kashgar (in China) had archbishops. All this took place hundreds of years before Canterbury gained its first archbishop. The Christian message spread far and wide. In these early days of the Church there were thriving Christian communities in Uzbekistan, Iran, Iraq, and many other places besides. The King of Yemen, for instance, converted to Christianity and a Greek-speaking visitor to Sri Lanka in about 550 found a community of Christians there as well.

Some of these Christian communities have remained unbroken to the present day. Indian Christians, for example, are proud of the fact that Saint Thomas brought Christianity to their country. The details of Saint Thomas's mission are hazy but recent historians have shown that there are good historical reasons for believing that Saint Thomas really did travel to and die in India, just as the other Apostles traveled widely in order to spread the good news of Jesus. Indian Christians are not alone in celebrating a Christian tradition that stretches back over one and a half thousand years; Iraqi Christians are also proud of the fact that Christianity came early to their country. By the mid-sixth century there were many Christians in places like Basra, Mosul, and Tikrit. Another Iraqi city, called Kokhe, which was very close to Baghdad, had so many Christians that it was served by five bishoprics.

The Syrian Church was also hugely important in the first Christian centuries. Saint Ephrem, one of the Doctors of the Church, came from Syria, and so too did a number of popes in the sixth and seventh centuries. Christianity was brought by the Apostles to Antioch, which is now in Turkey just across the border from Syria, though it was then an important Syrian city. It was in Antioch that the followers of Jesus were first called Christians, according to the Acts of the Apostles. Christianity then spread eastward from there, reaching Ctesiphon in modern-day Iraq less than a hundred years after the death of Christ and reaching Persia at a similar time. However, life was not straightforward for Christians in Persia, especially after AD 226 when Zoroastrianism was introduced as the state religion. Christians began to be persecuted and this period of persecution became particularly heavy when Christianity became the official religion of the Roman Empire.

Nonetheless, Christianity survived in the Persian Empire and began to flourish, not least because it was a missionary church. From the sixth century onward the head of the Church in the Persian Empire was the **Patriarch** of Seleucia-Ctesiphon, near Baghdad. He sent monks and other missionaries out across the whole of Asia, with the result being that 230 bishoprics and twenty-seven **metropolitan sees** were eventually set up. It was this Syriac-speaking Persian Church that seems to have brought Christianity to China as early as 625. So what is the evidence for Christianity in China at this very early date?

There is very clear and very impressive evidence, one piece of which was found in the early seventeenth century when some workers were digging the foundations of a building near Xian (where the famous Terracotta Army can be seen) and found an enormous slab of black marble called a stele. This stele (which weighed two tons and was nine feet high, three and a half feet wide, and a foot thick) was covered in writing which had been carved into the stone. There were 1,756 Chinese characters and seventy words in a language that neither the Chinese nor the European Jesuit priests to whom they showed it recognized. However, a picture of a cross emerging out of a lotus flower that had been carved at the top of the stele gave a clue to its origins. This was a Chinese Christian monument from the seventh century. And the strange writing was Syriac, recording the names of monks and bishops from the East Syrian Church. In other words, this was a Chinese Christian monument that demonstrated exactly how the faith had spread across the world.

What did the inscription say? Its heading was "Memorial of the introduction into China of the luminous religion from Syria." In other words, it was a stone document recording the arrival of Christianity in the country. The first section gives a summary of the Christian message in terms that would have seemed familiar to Chinese readers who knew Daoist teachings. The second section explains that when Alopen from the kingdom of Daqin (which probably means a bishop called Abraham from Persia) arrived in China he was welcomed by the Emperor Taizong who invited him to the palace at Xian. "The emperor had the holy books translated. In the library, within the forbidden doors, he inquired about the doctrine. He learned perfectly that [the doctrine] was correct and true and prescribed by special order that it be propagated." In other words, Christianity now had the backing of the emperor, even though he did not take the important step of converting to Christianity himself, as had happened in Ethiopia. Christian monasteries were immediately set up and Christianity took its place among the different religions then trying to make an impact in China.

However, the Xian stele is not the only evidence we have from this time. Even earlier documents have been found, including the Dunhuang Gloria. Dunhuang is a remarkable place. A huge complex of caves, it is the oldest surviving Buddhist site in China (and it is worth remembering that Buddhism is as much a "foreign" religion in China as Christianity is, having been brought to the country from India). It is also the site of one of the most remarkable archaeological discoveries of all time. In 1899 a Chinese Daoist monk stumbled on a hidden chamber that was packed with thousands of ancient manuscripts. Most of these were Buddhist documents but among them were some Christian documents, such as a few lines from Saint Paul's Epistle to the Galatians written in Syriac (and probably intended for use in a church lectionary) and a translation of the *Gloria in excelsis Deo*, known as the Dunhuang Gloria.

In addition, we have approximately thirty other Syrian Christian documents from China. Some of these were translated into Chinese as early as the 630s and 640s. One of these documents is called the *Sutra of Jesus the Messiah*. It is 206 verses long and is an attempt to explain the key truths of Christianity in terms that Buddhists would understand. Another document, the *Discourse of the Master of the World on Almsgiving*, is even longer. It explains that:

> Ten days after his Ascension, the Messiah again strengthened the faith of his disciples. He introduced them to the secret of the Way and gave them the Holy Breath.... Having received the Holy Breath, they had the power to teach about the Messiah to all nations and races of humanity and to reveal to the whole of humanity the judgment of the master of heaven.

Further on in the document, it explains that, "Although only 641 years have elapsed since the birth of the Messiah in his five elements, nevertheless he is known in all parts of the world." And that was certainly now the case. Christianity had spread a huge distance in a relatively short time.

Christianity has never been an exclusively western religion. It began in Israel and immediately spread eastward and southward as much as to the west. Of course, it also went northward too, though it took some years before places such as Russia and Poland, in the East, and England, in the West, were converted. The evidence from China also reminds us of the importance of many languages that we may not be familiar with in spreading the Christian message, including Aramaic and Syriac. It also reminds us that not all missionary effort was directed from the center. As we shall see, England was converted in large part because of an initiative launched by a great pope in Rome, but China received the gospel initially from Persia. The Church has always been proudly catholic; globalization is not an exclusively modern phenomenon.

# CHAPTER 13

## Saint Antony and the Desert Fathers

LET'S TRAVEL NOW TO A VERY DIFFERENT part of the Roman Empire. When the Emperor Decius persecuted Christians in the mid-third century, some people fled to the deserts of Egypt. There they became hermits, men and women who lived apart from the world and led a life of prayer and penance. The most important of these people was Saint Antony who lived from about 251 to 356 and who became well known when Saint Athanasius, the Bishop of Alexandria in Egypt, wrote a book about him.

Saint Athanasius tells us that Antony, who came from Egypt, was "the son of well-born and devout parents." He also tells us, more surprisingly, that "while he was still a boy he refused to learn to read and write or join in the silly games of the other little children; instead he burned with a desire for God and lived a life of simplicity at home." This pious childhood was interrupted by two important events: the death of his parents when he was about eighteen years old and the moment when he walked into a church and heard this passage being read: "If you would be perfect, go, sell what you possess and give to the poor, and you will have treasure in heaven; and come, follow me" (Mt 19:21).

Antony was struck to the core by this Gospel passage but rather than rush straight into the desert to become a monk, he first sold his possessions and, crucially, made sure that his sister was well provided for. Gradually he moved further and further away from the comfortable life he had grown up with. Having given all his money to the poor, he withdrew to a place nearby to live a simple life of manual work and prayer. From there he moved to a more remote place—a tomb, in fact—where he lived for a few more years before finally moving into the desert itself at the age of thirty-five. There he lived until the ripe old age of 105, having influenced a whole generation of Christians who looked to his example of self-sacrificing simplicity.

Saint Antony was certainly not the only Christian to seek God and the way of radical discipleship in the desert. Another important figure was Saint Pachomius, who became such a popular hermit that a large group of disciples gathered around him. Realizing that he wouldn't be able to live out the rest of his life in solitude, he drew up a set of rules for his followers and created one of the first monasteries. Saint Pachomius's *Rule* was highly influential and was soon copied across the Roman Empire.

Hermits and monks like Saint Antony and Saint Pachomius attracted a massive following and, to use a modern phrase, became mainstream. Because the desert fathers, as they became known, influenced important figures in the early Church, such as Saint Basil, Saint Athanasius, and Saint Augustine (who drew up his own highly influential Rule), monasticism soon spread to the cities.

An important person in this development was Saint Martin of Tours who was, in fact, born in Hungary. From an early age, he "longed for the desert" but his father had different ideas. He was determined that the young Martin should have a military career. Eventually, Martin managed to leave the army and promptly went off to live in a hermit's cell in Milan. Forced out of the city by the Arians, he moved to the island of Gallinara off the Italian coast with another monk. From there he moved to Poitiers in modern-day France but his desire to be a humble monk was again disrupted, this time because he was chosen to be Bishop of Tours. Even so, Martin refused to change his way of life completely. While carrying out his duties as bishop he lived initially in a simple cell next to his cathedral before seeking a more isolated cell outside the city. There he was joined by many others who were impressed by his life. Without ever planning to do so, Martin found himself at the center of a monastic community.

While Saint Martin, Saint Augustine, and others were establishing monastic communities in the towns and cities where they lived, other men and women were still traveling to the desert to live a life of extreme poverty and simplicity. To our modern eyes, the behavior of some of these monks and hermits seems very surprising indeed. From the fifth century onward, some of them lived at the top of tall pillars; in fact the most famous of all, Saint Simeon Stylites, lived on top of a pillar for the last thirty-seven years of his life, so great was his desire for solitude. Simeon Stylites certainly had an unusual lifestyle but we shouldn't look at his behavior out of context. The reason the desert fathers were so popular was because they met a need. They offered practical wisdom and a radical example that appealed to many people from across the Roman Empire.

What sort of practical wisdom? Wisdom like this:

Somebody asked Antony, "What shall I do in order to please God?" He replied, "Do what I tell you, which is this: wherever you go, keep God in mind; whatever you do, follow the example of holy Scripture; wherever you are, stay there and do not move away in a hurry. If you keep to these guidelines, you will be saved."

The Desert Fathers packed a lot of carefully considered advice into apparently simple comments. Imagine the restless soul who had traveled to the desert to speak to Antony only to be told that there was no need to come to the desert; he could live with God wherever he was.

Here's another pretty good piece of advice: "A hermit said, 'All chatter is unnecessary. Nowadays everyone talks but what is needed is action. This is what God wants, not useless talking.'" That suggestion may have been made hundreds of years ago but it is still highly relevant today.

And here's another lovely example from a respected Egyptian monk which reminds us that, despite the terribly harsh conditions in which these monks and nuns lived, they had a very deep understanding of human needs: "If I see my brother going to sleep [while saying his prayers], I shall take his head and lay it gently on my lap."

An extraordinary range of people became hermits, monks, and nuns: uneducated peasants, traders, noblemen, former prostitutes, Romans, Egyptians, and sub-Saharan Africans. The monastic movement drew on precisely the same groups of people Jesus had associated with during his lifetime. One of the most famous monks in the fourth century, for example, was John the Dwarf. He was born into a poor Egyptian family and moved into the desert when he was about eighteen years old. He became so famous that he lived in an underground cave so that he could get the peace and quiet he needed to draw close to God in prayer. Another Egyptian monk was Macarius the Great who was a camel driver before he became a monk. An impressive CV was not needed to become a great monk or hermit.

However, not all monks and nuns were from humble backgrounds. Paula was a noble Roman lady who, when her husband died, became a nun, traveling with her daughter to Saint Jerome's monastery in Bethlehem. Arsenius had a similar background. He came from a high-ranking family in Rome and was a friend of the Emperor Theodosius. Leaving all this privilege behind, he traveled from Rome when he was in his mid-thirties and sailed to Egypt, where he became a disciple of John the Dwarf.

At a time when it was the educated elite who became bishops and archbishops, the Desert Fathers were drawn from a much broader spectrum of society. As we shall see, it was these hermits, monks, and nuns who launched a new chapter in the life of the Church when the Roman Empire started to collapse around them. But before we look at that collapse we need to travel a little further down the Nile, to the city of the sharp-nosed fish.

## CHAPTER 14

# *The City of the Sharp-Nosed Fish*

IN 1897 TWO ARCHAEOLOGISTS FROM Oxford started digging into some sand-covered mounds in the Egyptian desert. What they found were rubbish dumps belonging to a city called Oxyrhynchos, which means the city of the sharp-nosed fish, but these were not just any old rubbish dumps; they contained tens of thousands of fragments of **papyrus**.

Bernard Grenfell and Arthur Hunt were young men looking around for a new area of research. They knew that papyrus had been found in Egypt, preserved in the bone-dry desert in a way that would not have been possible in the damper climates of Greece or Rome, or even in the Nile delta in Egypt itself. The next question was where exactly to look. The spot they hit upon looked distinctly unpromising at first. Half the area was covered by a village and the other half, according to Grenfell, was something of a mess:

> A thousand years' use as a quarry for limestone and bricks had clearly reduced the buildings and houses to utter ruin.... Of the walls themselves scarcely anything was left, except part of the town wall, enclosing the north-west of the site, the buildings having been cleared away down to their foundations

They started by excavating the cemetery but didn't make any great discoveries. Then they turned their attention to a low mound. Almost immediately they found a page from the apocryphal Gospel of Thomas, then they found part of Saint Matthew's Gospel. Then they found more and more and more. Over the course of the next three months they found enough papyri to fill 280 boxes: "The flow of papyri soon became a torrent it was difficult to keep pace with," they wrote.

Of course, Grenfell and Hunt didn't do this work on their own. They hired local workers, the majority of whom were boys. ("[N]early every boy in the district who could walk wanted to be taken on to the work.") The most impressive of these workers, according to Grenfell, was an eight-year old called Sabr' Said, "who had a wonderful eye for the right kind of soil for finding papyri." It is worth remembering that some of the greatest archaeological finds of recent times were made by a young boy.

Despite these remarkable finds, Grenfell and Hunt moved onto another site, only returning to Oxyrhynchos six years later. Again they found thousands of pieces of papyrus. Employing over a hundred workers and working in extremely windy conditions, which were liable to sweep away their precious discoveries, they ploughed on. In 1905 they discovered a basketful of literary papyrus rolls, most of which had been torn up before being thrown away on the ancient rubbish dump. However, the task of piecing it all back again was well worth it. There were texts by Plato and Thucydides, as well as poems by Pindar, one of Euripides' plays (Hypsipyle), and other works that had not been seen since the classical era.

After ten years work they had collected 700 boxes of papyri. But when I write "boxes," don't imagine anything too grand. Those boxes included an old biscuit tin and recycled kerosene containers. They also found many other objects, including coins, a mold for counterfeiting coins, dice, keys, combs, tweezers, socks, slippers, dolls (some of which were made out of papyrus), a birdtrap, and "some loaves of Roman bread, in appearance much resembling Hot Cross buns."

Over the next hundred years and even into the present day, historians have worked hard to piece the fragments of papyrus together and, in so doing, they have discovered all sorts of documents, including one of Aristotle's lost books. They have also discovered a great deal about everything from families and schools to religion and poetry. A friend of mine wrote his PhD thesis on what you could discover about the Romans' food supply from the fragments. The desert sands of Egypt preserved the Roman past as well as Vesuvius's volcanic mud and ash.

So, what can we learn about this city? Let's look at a letter from a schoolboy to his father found among the papyrus fragments: "To my lord father Arion, Thonis sends greetings," he starts. "Before all else I make a supplication for you every day, praying also that I may recover you in good health and all our people, before the ancestral gods where I am a guest."

So far so polite (though he does go on to complain that his father hasn't written or visited him). It's the ending I particularly like: "I send greetings also to my teachers. Good health, my lord father, and, I pray, good fortune to you for many years, along with my brothers (may the evil eye not touch them!). P. S. Remember our pigeons."

Speaking of pigeons, another letter mentions sending a box of grapes to a child's tutor, or "the bay pigeons and other small birds that I don't usually eat.... Anything at all that I didn't eat...send to my daughter's tutor, so that he takes pains with her." Sadly we may never know how effective these little gifts were.

What we get from these papyri is an inkling of what it must have been like to have lived in this particular city 2000 years ago and, just occasionally, what we learn is very disturbing. In a letter to his wife in 1 BC, for example, a man from Oxyrhynchos, wrote: "Hilarion to Alis heartiest greetings, and to my dear Berous and Apollonarion. Know that we are still even now in Alexandria. Do not worry if when all the others return I remain in Alexandria. I beg and beseech of you to take care of the little child, and as soon as we receive wages I will send them to you. If—good luck to you!—you bear offspring, if it is a male, let it live; if it is a female, expose it." We will return to the subject of children being abandoned in a later chapter to gain an insight into ancient attitudes toward the family.

Gradually Oxyrhynchos changed. By the end of the fourth century it was a Christian city and was famous for its monasteries. This is what one visitor wrote: "We also visited Oxyrhynchos, a city in the Thebaid, whose wonders beggar description. So full is it of monasteries inside that the monks themselves make the walls resound, and it is surrounded outside by other monasteries, so that there is another city outside the city." According to the same visitor, there were 10,000 monks and 20,000 nuns in one area alone, though the figures may not be wholly accurate.

Another intriguing piece of papyrus from the rubbish heap dated AD 325 tells us that a court case was to be postponed "until after the Lord's Day." Taking Sunday off may not seem so surprising but it would have been a new idea to the people of the city because working on the Christian Sabbath was only banned in AD 321 after Constantine came to power. The world was changing and Oxyrhynchos was changing with it. However, it was about to change even more; the empire itself was under threat.

# CHAPTER 15

## *The End That Never Was*

HISTORY SEEMS PRETTY STRAIGHTFORWARD. All you have to do is find the facts and the past sorts itself out into a story we can all understand. Or so we might hope. But, of course, it's not nearly as straightforward as that. Even when historians have the facts, their interpretations can vary dramatically, and even establishing the facts can be surprisingly tricky. Take the end of the Roman Empire, for instance. You might have thought that finding out when the Roman Empire ended would be easy, but it isn't.

The standard story is that during the fourth century AD the Roman Empire came under increasing pressure from barbarian tribes like the Huns, the Goths, and the Vandals. Forced to concentrate on defending Rome and the center of the empire, the Romans withdrew troops from outlying provinces such as Britain but, despite their best efforts, the empire eventually came crashing down either in AD 410 when Rome was **sacked** by the Visigoths or in AD 476 when the Vandals took over.

But there's one basic problem with this version of history. It's wrong. The Roman Empire didn't collapse in 410 or in 476. As we've seen, there was a lot more to the Roman Empire than Rome itself, so the empire didn't come crashing down just because Rome had been overrun by a barbarian tribe. Rome was important and its capture was a huge blow but Rome was no longer the capital of the empire; Constantinople was. And Constantinople was not overrun by barbarians. So the Roman Empire continued, even though it was now a much smaller empire than it had previously been.

So if the Roman Empire didn't collapse in the fifth century when did it end? The answer is 1453 when Constantinople was conquered by the Ottoman Turks. In other words, the usual date that schoolchildren have been taught is out by a thousand years.

How could historians have got the date so horribly wrong? One answer is that lots of them didn't. When they were being careful, historians wrote that the end of the western Roman Empire came in the fifth century. But even today if you look for books about the Romans, you will find that the majority of them contain nothing at all about the empire during the last thousand years of its existence.

This really matters. Book after book tells us that the Romans worshiped many gods, that they spoke Latin, and that they watched gladiators fight each other to the death. All this is true, but it's only partially true. The Roman Empire was also Christian for over a thousand years. For over a thousand years Greek was at least as important as Latin. And, for a thousand years, gladiatorial shows were illegal. In a court of law we have to swear to tell the truth, the whole truth, and nothing but the truth. When it comes to the Romans, we often get the truth but rarely the whole truth.

So back to the question of how historians got the dates so wrong. One explanation is that historians in the West didn't know so much about the Greek-speaking, Eastern half of the empire and because they didn't know so much about it they didn't take it so seriously. They called it the Byzantine Empire, which is very misleading, partly because the people who lived there still called it the Roman Empire and partly because the capital of the empire was now called Constantinople rather than Byzantium.

It is also possible that historians studied what happened in Roman Britain and subconsciously saw it as the norm rather than as the exception. The Roman legions left Britain in AD 410 and never came back. There is still a huge amount of debate about what Roman Britain was like in the years after the Roman troops left but everyone is agreed that Britain, more than almost any other part of the empire, eventually became a thoroughly un-Roman place. For a start, the country became largely pagan again when the people we now call Anglo-Saxons invaded (even though "Anglo-Saxon" is an anachronism). Latin all but died out. Roman towns were abandoned. It even got to the stage where Anglo-Saxon poets could look at the remains of Roman buildings and wonder if they were the work of giants. It's perhaps no surprise then that British historians should have focused on the collapse of the Roman Empire rather than on its survival in many other parts of the Western world.

When barbarian tribes overran Italy, it was the end of *a* world, not the end of *the* world, the end of *a* civilization, not the end of civilization as a whole. The Roman Empire received a mauling but it wasn't long before the emperors in Constantinople started fighting back. But before we look at the fightback, we need to look at the life and work of a man who was at the sharp end of the barbarian incursions and who, more than anyone else, came to grips with what they meant for the Christian world he was now part of.

# CHAPTER 16

# Saint Augustine and the City of God

AT THE END OF THE FOURTH CENTURY, Christianity seemed pretty secure. Except during Emperor Julian's brief reign, Christians had been able to relax, knowing that their religion was no longer illegal and that great ecumenical councils were sorting out some of the problems caused by heretics within the Church. Then in AD 393 the Emperor Theodosius proclaimed Christianity the only legal religion in the empire. Christians might have been forgiven for thinking that they'd never had it so good.

Most people in the empire were now Christians and only two groups really held out. Some people in the countryside still clung to their old pagan beliefs, as did some intellectuals. But missionary efforts continued and there seemed no reason to doubt that both groups would eventually come round.

Then the Visigoths invaded Italy and sacked Rome in AD 410 as we have already seen. The great traditional capital of the Roman Empire was all but destroyed. It was a disaster and people looked around for someone to blame. For pagan intellectuals the obvious target was the Church. They argued that Christians had weakened the empire, that they had brought down the wrath of the gods and now the gods had allowed Rome itself to be sacked.

This was a troubling argument but one Christian leader was more than equal to the challenge. Saint Augustine, the bishop of Hippo, a city in what is now

Algeria in North Africa, wrote one of the greatest books of all time to answer the Christians' critics. It was called *The City of God*.

Augustine was fifty-six years old when he started writing the book and seventy-two when he finished it. Why did it take him so long? Part of the reason is that he had a lot to say. I have a copy of the book in front of me now and it is over 1,000 pages long. Right at the start of the book, Augustine says that he has a *magnum opus et arduum*, a long and difficult job to do. He knew that the task he had set himself was a really tricky one that would take years to complete, especially as he had many other calls on his time. However, the fact that he was prepared to take so long over the writing of the book also tells us about the kind of book he wanted it to be.

On the one hand, it was clearly a response to a current crisis. And what a crisis, too. Saint Jerome spoke for many when he said that "the city that had conquered the whole world had itself been conquered." To many Roman citizens this was much more than the destruction of a city; it was like the end of the world. But, on the other hand, Augustine knew that there were bigger issues at stake. Bigger even than the possible end of the Roman Empire. The fall of Rome raised questions about how God works in history and about the kind of world he wants on earth. You can't answer questions like those overnight; Augustine needed time to spell out a truly Christian understanding of history.

*The City of God* is a long book and a summary won't do it justice, but what Augustine explains is that life on earth is a mixture of joys and disasters, and that good and bad people alike are affected by blessings and catastrophes. This was true when the Roman Empire worshipped the pagan gods and true when the Romans turned to Christ. The fall of Rome to the Visigoths was, therefore, just one more disaster and couldn't be explained by a change of religion. Instead, Augustine suggested another way of interpreting history. His argument was that there are two cities, the earthly and the heavenly, and that true happiness can only be found in preparing ourselves for the heavenly one. Because we are exiles here on earth, we should not be surprised or dismayed by disasters, even disasters as great as the Visigoth invasion. Our true home is to be found in the heavenly city, which will never be attacked or destroyed.

Augustine's book met a specific need at the time he wrote it but his ideas have continued to resonate throughout Christian history and have helped shape Christian theology. As we shall see in later chapters, Christianity is quite different from other religions in its attitudes toward politics. At the heart of Islam, for example, is the idea that there should be no separation between the religious and political authorities. Muhammad and his successors, who were known as caliphs, were religious and political (and often military) leaders of Islam. By contrast, the pope's political role and the emperor's religious role were very limited in Christianity. There were times when popes took too much political power and times when emperors took too much religious control but, after Augustine, there was never any doubt that the two had separate roles.

This idea that the Church and the State had separate roles is sometimes called secularity. The job of the State—the job of emperors and kings—is to keep the peace, dispense justice, and maintain good order in society. The job of the Church, by contrast, is to help people come to know God and so find salvation. There are times when the two jobs overlap but they are different jobs.

This notion of secularity rests on a particular understanding of faith and reason. According to the Church certain things have been revealed by God and other things can be worked out by human reason. The Church doesn't tell scientists, footballers, or even teachers how to do their job because they can work it out for themselves. What's more, they can become saints by doing these jobs well and to the glory of God; they don't have to give up their day job and become a monk in order to grow closer to God.

Saint Augustine understood this well. That's why he wrote commentaries on the Scriptures, to explain what had been revealed by God, as well as works of philosophy that relied on human reason. Saint Augustine and other Church Fathers realized they didn't have to reject the work of the pagan Greek and Roman philosophers who had gone before them. Instead they could build on their work, drawing on the new insights that Christian revelation had given them.

We see this in another book by Saint Augustine: his *Confessions*. This book is a kind of spiritual autobiography, the most detailed and intimate autobiography of ancient times, in which he describes his Christian mother and pagan father, his misspent youth, his education, his attraction to different pagan philosophies, and then his conversion to Christianity under the influence of another great Christian leader of the time, Saint Ambrose of Milan.

In the *Confessions*, Augustine writes about the attraction of Neo-Platonic ideas, the ideas of philosophers who had developed Plato's philosophy. Augustine explained that the Neo-Platonists had saved him from some errors and so helped him on his way to the fullness of the truth that he found in Christianity. Platonic ideas were therefore a preparation for the Gospel, a *praeparatio evangelii.*

In his *City of God*, Saint Augustine answered Christianity's pagan critics but one of his great strengths was that he was able to see the True, the Good, and the Beautiful in the best of the pre-Christian writers as well and, in so doing, he helped ensure that Christianity survived long after the Visigoths, the Vandals, and even the Romans had disappeared into the mists of history.

# CHAPTER 17

# Family Life and the Kindness of Strangers

AN INTERESTING, BUT SURPRISINGLY COM-plicated, question that might have occurred to you is this: what difference did Christianity make to the Roman Empire? How far did the empire change as a result of the change of religion?

The reason it's complicated is that fundamental changes happen very slowly, especially in a place as large as the Roman Empire. Some things did change very quickly—Sunday became a legal holiday, establishing the practice that we still have today; churches were built across the empire; and the execution of Christians came to a halt—but other aspects of Roman life took much longer to change. Gladiatorial shows were banned in AD 326, for example, but we know from Saint Augustine's *Confessions* that they were still taking place in Rome as late as the 380s. However, eventually, as Christianity took root in the empire, gladiatorial shows died out.

Family life also changed slowly as Christian ideas gradually took hold at a deep level. There have always been families but what people mean by the family and how they regard the family has changed dramatically over time. For pre-Christian Romans the *familia* included not just parents and children but slaves too, and the *paterfamilias* (father of the family) had absolute power over them all. Romans seem to have taken it for granted that the father had the right to execute even his adult children if necessary.

Even after marriage, a Roman woman remained part of her father's *familia* (though her children did not). Women could own their own property and, with their father's permission, obtain a divorce (even if her husband didn't want one). However, this apparent freedom came at a cost: a woman's children were no longer legally hers after divorce.

Historians sometimes write as though women in the past had no rights at all, but the truth is that what women were and weren't able to do varied greatly over time and in different societies. When the Greeks conquered Egypt under Alexander the Great, for example, they were surprised to find that Egyptian women could move around freely without veils, since respectable women in Greece were expected to cover their head in public (if they made public appearances at all). Women also had unexpected legal rights in Ancient Egypt. We have a piece of papyrus from 249 BC, for example, which explains that a woman "loaned her husband 273 grams of silver at thirty percent interest, to be paid back within three years as was usual." The role of women in Roman families also changed over the years, especially with the coming of Christianity. According to one historian, "the older vision of Roman family life based on the legal powers of the *paterfamilias* gave way to a new ideal, in which the *paterfamilias* had essentially ceded to the Christian bishop his role of arbiter in matters of piety and justice." This historian argues that gradually the idea of marriage as a commitment for life became established because of the coming of Christianity.

As time went on the ban on divorce that Constantine had set in motion became further established. It was undoubtedly women who benefitted from this legal change as they were far more likely to be set aside by their husbands under the previous law code than they were to exercise their own right to divorce. As the law was slowly Christianized, they gained legal protection against **arbitrary** divorce from unscrupulous husbands.

Alongside these legal changes came a new view of women as "soldiers of Christ whose persistence in virtue would crush the armies of Satan," as one historian put it. Women were not viewed as second-class citizens with no role of their own; they could now be Christian wives and mothers with very clear roles to play in what was increasingly a dangerous world. Crucially, under Christian influence, the wife was no longer seen as part of her father's family but, with her husband and children, formed a new family unit, and as wife and mother in that new family unit she had a certain authority that she had never had before.

Another fundamental change was in the way that unmarried people were regarded. Before Constantine became emperor, the unmarried were clearly discriminated against in the Roman empire (which had big implications for Christians who from a very early date believed that priests and bishops should not marry). Cicero wrote about the fines that unmarried people had to pay and another Roman writer, Livy, explained that special privileges were granted to parents who had three children (or four if they were freedmen). Choosing not to marry would have baffled most Romans but Christianity offered a new ideal: the ideal of unmarried men and women dedicating themselves to Christ.

Christianity brought changes to family life as it did to every other aspect of society but there were some surprising continuities as well. The leading historian of child abandonment and adoption for this period of history has written that "children were abandoned throughout Europe from Hellenistic antiquity to the end of the Middle Ages in great numbers, by parents of every social standing, in a great variety of circumstances."

Although many of the early Church Fathers argued strongly against this relatively widespread practice of child abandonment, the unintended consequence of the triumph of Christianity may actually have been an increase in the numbers of children being abandoned by their parents, partly because it was obvious to all that churches and monasteries were prepared to take them in.

This widespread abandonment of children sounds rather grim — and, of course, it was — but there is also a lot of evidence that "the 'kindness of strangers' . . . seems to have been sufficient to rescue most abandoned children." Abandonment was widespread, but so too was adoption. At the very heart of Rome, on the Capitoline Hill overlooking the forum, was a statue of a wolf suckling Romulus and Remus, the mythical founders of Rome. According to Roman legend the abandoned baby twins were found and suckled by the wolf and then adopted by a shepherd and his wife, before going on to found Rome itself. With a founding myth like this, it is no surprise that adoption should have been regarded so favorably in the Roman world.

Another important question we need to consider is how long people tended to live at this point in history. Unfortunately, it is very difficult to find out because there is so little evidence. **Census** records from Egypt during the early years of the Roman Empire suggest that if girls reached the age of ten they could expect to live, on average, to the age of thirty-five. Average life expectancy for women (taking into account the many people who died at birth or in childhood) was probably closer to twenty-two. We can also look at skeletons in excavated cemeteries for evidence. From these skeletons we can estimate that in the Roman Empire as a whole (between AD 100 and 200) women lived to the age of thirty-five on average. In Britain in AD 100 women seem to have lived on average to the age of forty-five.

These Roman skeletons also provide evidence for the number of children a woman might have had, the average being 3.3 per woman in the year AD 120 (though the skeletons recovered from Herculaneum suggest an average of only 1.8 children per woman). No doubt the number of children varied greatly from family to family but the lack of strong evidence and the almost complete absence of children from written records means that we will never be absolutely certain about family size in the Roman Empire. There is still a great deal we have to learn.

# CHAPTER 18

# Were the Barbarians Barbarians?

IN HIS *HISTORY OF THE ENGLISH CHURCH and People*, Saint Bede the Venerable tells us that Britain was invaded by three tribes after the Romans left: the Angles, the Saxons, and the Jutes. You may well have heard about the Angles and the Saxons, but what about the Jutes?

The real surprise is that we know nothing about them apart from what Bede tells us, which is very little. Much the same is true—though not quite to the same degree—with many of the other so-called barbarian tribes that caused the Romans such difficulties. We are not entirely sure where many of them came from, who led them, or what they hoped to achieve with their attacks. In a world dominated by the Internet, we often assume that we can find an answer to every question by Googling, but the truth is that much of the past is still lost to us. So let's look at what we do know.

Firstly, we know that the barbarians weren't really barbarians. The word "barbarian" is a term of abuse; as the sound suggests, it was a word coined by the Greeks to describe outsiders, people who sounded (to them) like sheep. Barbarians were seen as uncultured and illiterate thugs. Now, it is true that the Burgundians referred to themselves as barbarians in the Burgundian Code (an important set of laws from the sixth century), but the very fact that this code of laws exists suggests the very opposite. The Burgundians (and after them the Franks and other so-called barbarian tribes) created complex legal systems that built upon what they had inherited or learned from the Romans. What's more, the Burgundian

Code was written in Latin, which is hardly evidence of barbarity. It is true that many Burgundians were **illiterate** but that did not automatically make them barbarians in the negative sense it is usually given.

What about religion? Because we know that the Anglo-Saxons were pagans at first, it is easy to assume that the same was true elsewhere in Europe. In one sense, of course, it was. Christianity was still a young religion and so it's hardly a surprise that it took a long time before the barbarian tribes were converted to Christianity but, in another sense, it wasn't true at all. The majority of the barbarian tribes that attacked the Roman Empire had bishops, priests, and churches of their own. Most of them were Arians.

As we have seen, the Church tried to deal with Arianism at the Council of Nicaea in AD 325 but Arianism lingered for many more years—in fact, for many centuries—partly because the Visigoths, Burgundians, and Ostrogoths rejected the Catholic doctrines that had been accepted at Nicaea and accepted Arian ones instead. They were heretical Christians rather than pagans.

So, what we've seen is that the so-called barbarians were not wholly illiterate, nor wholly pagan, nor wholly without laws. But were they wholly violent? It certainly wasn't a peaceful era. As one historian of Anglo-Saxon England put it, peace sometimes broke out. However, it is too simplistic to see the barbarians as violent invaders and the Greeks and Romans as peace-loving cultural heroes. The Roman Empire existed only because it had been conquered by the Romans and many of the barbarian tribes got a toe-hold in the Roman Empire in the first place, not because they invaded but because the Romans employed them to keep other barbarian tribes out. Later some of these Roman employees (to use a rather **anachronistic** expression) took advantage of weaknesses in the Roman Empire to seize territory for themselves. Some of them simply weren't paid and so decided that they had better seize the compensation they were owed.

Eventually different barbarian tribes managed to take over different parts of the Western Roman Empire. It got pretty complicated but if you want a list of names and places, here it goes. The Huns attacked Gaul and Italy. The Visigoths attacked Rome and then took over much of France and some of Spain. The Ostrogoths set up a powerful kingdom in what we now call Italy. The Vandals and the Moors took over much of North Africa. The Franks and the Burgundians overran Gaul. The Angles, Saxons, and Jutes took over Britain.

However, this makes it all too neat. The reality was much messier. When we talk about the Romans, we need to remember that what we actually mean is all the people in the Roman Empire, most of whom had very little to do with Rome itself. In fact, one of the main reasons the Romans were so successful is that they managed to persuade the people they conquered that they should want to be like the Romans too. The rulers of the conquered tribes soon wanted baths, theatres, philosophy, and everything else that went into making Rome what it was.

In much the same way, the barbarian tribes aped the Romans. Quite often they wanted recognition from the Roman emperor even when they were seizing his territory. So when we say that the Ostrogoths ruled Italy, what we really mean is that a relatively few Ostrogoths (who were probably quite difficult to distinguish from the Visigoths or any of the other tribes) ruled over a mass of people who still regarded themselves as Romans and who hankered after the glory days of the empire. All of which means that we are not a great deal closer to understanding what the barbarians were really like. To do that we need to look closely at their hair.

Let's start by looking at some laws from the Burgundian Code that we mentioned earlier. Here are some of the punishments set out by law:

> If anyone seizes a native freeman violently by the hair, if with one hand, let him pay two **solidi**; if with both hands, four solidi; moreover, let the fine be set at six solidi.

> If anyone seizes a freedman or another's slave violently by the hair, either with one hand or both, it is pleasing that determination of punishment be made.

> Whoever unintentionally provides a native freeman or slave who is a fugitive with false hair, let him forfeit five solidi; if he provides him with such hair intentionally, let him pay the **wergeld** of the fleeing man.

> If any native freewoman has her hair cut off and is humiliated without cause (when innocent) by any native freeman in her home or on the road, and this can be proved with witnesses, let the doer of the deed pay her twelve solidi, and let the amount of the fine be twelve solidi.

> If any native freeman presumes to cut off the hair of a native freewoman in her courtyard, we order that he pay thirty solidi to the woman, and let the fine be twelve solidi. But if the woman has gone forth from her courtyard to fight, and her hair has been cut off or she has received wounds, let it

be her fault because she has gone forth from her home; and let nothing be sought from him who struck her or cut her hair.

If any Jew presumes to raise a hand against a Christian with fist, shoe, club, whip, or stone, or has seized his hair, let him be condemned to the loss of a hand.

You're probably beginning to get the idea: hair was important to the Burgundians, though we should also remember that there were plenty of laws that had nothing to do with hair at all.

What can we learn from these laws that focus on hair crimes? Firstly, we can see that punishment revolved around compensation rather than around prison, and the amount of compensation—known as wergeld or wergild—was very precisely worked out for each crime. The reason the Burgundians paid so much attention to compensation was to prevent people from simply taking revenge on each other. It may seem rather crude to us but the Burgundian law code was designed to put an end to one of the curses of barbarian society: the blood feud.

The barbarian tribes that now dominated Europe were used to violence and instant justice. If a member of one family was killed, his relatives saw it as their duty to kill the murderer (or, failing that, a member of his family). That family would then seek revenge in turn. This cycle of violence could continue for years or even generations, with catastrophic consequences for society as a whole. The Burgundian Law Code was one of several attempts to replace this system with a less bloody approach.

The second point to notice is that it wasn't just the rich and powerful who were protected by the law.

Women and slaves also received protection, though it is also true that they did not have the same rights as freemen. Indeed, discrimination was built into the legal code, as we can see from the last law which clearly distinguishes between the treatment Jews and Christians received.

The final point is that hair was important not because it looked nice but because it was a status symbol in Burgundian society. If you had long hair you were a person of some importance, which is one reason why providing someone with false hair was a crime. We can see this in the life of Saint Clotilde, a Burgundian princess who married into the royal family of the Franks (the **Merovingians**) and who converted her husband, Clovis, from Arianism to Catholicism. After her husband's death, Clotilde tried to protect her grandchildren from the political ambitions of two of her unscrupulous children. Despite her best efforts these grandchildren were taken captive by her sons who then sent her a message without words. They sent her a sword and a pair of scissors. In other words, the message was that the grandchildren had to choose between having their hair cut off or being killed. According to one account, Clotilde was so angry that she said she would rather have them killed and that, in fact, is what happened.

What on earth was going on? How could anyone make such an apparently ludicrous decision? Why might anyone have preferred death to a haircut? As we have seen, Clotilde married into the Merovingian dynasty and the Merovingians are sometimes known as the long-haired kings. This is what distinguished them from their neighbors. Their long hair marked them out as rulers. So when Clotilde's grandchildren were threatened with the prospect of having their hair cut off, they were facing more than a chilly head;

they were being threatened with a total loss of political power. Their uncles were declaring that they were going to rule Gaul instead of them. Faced with this political coup, Clotilde may well have said that she would rather have them dead than deprived of their rightful political position.

Now is that the sort of story you were expecting when you read that we were going to be looking at hair?

# CHAPTER 19

# Boethius, Cassiodorus, and the Liberal Arts

WHILE CLOTILDE WAS TRYING TO PROTECT her grandchildren in what is now France, the Ostrogoths were in charge of what later became Italy. What had once been the very heart of the Roman Empire was now ruled by a barbarian king. Did this mean that the great world of learning that the Romans had created had gone up in flames? Not quite.

There were some very interesting people still working for the Ostrogothic king in Ravenna, the capital of the Ostrogothic kingdom. One of these was a man called Boethius. He was particularly important because he realized the importance of preserving the best of Greek learning in the West and so set about translating the works of Plato and Aristotle into Latin.

Now, what's all this got to do with the liberal arts?

The liberal arts formed the basis of Roman education for many hundreds of years. Over the years Roman thinkers and teachers developed a very clear idea of what the most important parts of a curriculum should be. Many children were taught what became known as the Trivium and the Quadrivium. The Trivium meant logic, grammar and rhetoric, and the Quadrivium meant arithmetic, geometry, astronomy, and music.

What this meant in practice was not what you might imagine. Saint Isidore of Seville, writing in the early seventh century, defined these subjects in this way:

There are seven disciplines of the liberal arts. The first is grammar, that is, skill in speaking. The second is rhetoric, which, on account of the brilliance and fluency of its **eloquence**, is considered most necessary in public proceedings. The third is dialectic, otherwise known as logic, which separates the true from the false by very subtle argumentation. The fourth is arithmetic, which contains the principles and classifications of numbers. The fifth is music, which consists of poems and songs. The sixth is geometry, which encompasses the measures and dimensions of the earth. The seventh is astronomy, which covers the law of the stars.

In order to teach these topics, books were needed, especially books written by scholars like Boethius who had a really good grounding in Greek as well as in Latin. Unfortunately, Boethius was accused by the Ostrogothic king, Theodoric, almost certainly unjustly, of plotting with the Roman emperor in Constantinople and was imprisoned for a year, after which he was tortured and executed. Curiously, it is this period of imprisonment for which Boethius is now chiefly remembered because it was while he was in prison that he wrote possibly his greatest work, *The Consolation of Philosophy*.

Boethius may have been one of the last great writers and thinkers in the West to have a strong grasp of both Latin and Greek but the liberal arts certainly didn't die with him. In fact, if anything they spread much more widely after his death and most of the credit for this can be given to a man who tried and failed to set up a school: Cassiodorus.

Cassiodorus also worked for the Ostrogoths and in his most important book, the *Institutions of Divine and Secular Learning*, he gives a vivid picture of what life was like at the time when Boethius was being put to death:

> When I realized that there was such a zealous and eager pursuit of secular learning, by which the majority of mankind hopes to obtain knowledge of the world, I was deeply grieved, I admit, that Holy Scripture should so lack public teachers, whereas secular authors certainly flourish in widespread teaching. Together with blessed Pope Agapetus of Rome, I made efforts to collect money so that it should rather be the Christian schools in the city of Rome that could employ learned teachers... from whom the faithful might gain eternal salvation for their souls and the adornment of sober and pure eloquence for their speech. They say that such a system existed for a long time at Alexandria and that the Hebrews are now using it enthusiastically in Nisbis, a city of Syria. But since I could not accomplish this task because of raging wars and violent struggles in the Kingdom of Italy... I was moved by divine love to devise for you, with God's help, these introductory books to take the place of a teacher.

We can learn a great deal about sixth-century Italy even from these few sentences. We can see that there was an education system but that it was affected by "raging wars and violent struggles." We can see that the pope and a government official were working together to improve Christian education. We can gain an understanding of what Cassiodorus saw to be the purpose of education: "eternal salvation for [the pupils'] souls and the adornment of sober and pure eloquence for their speech." And, finally, we can see that the balance of

power had shifted to the East, with Cassiodorus looking
to Syria for an example of a good school.

What may be less clear is the context in which this
book was written. By this stage in his career, Cassiodorus had retired to a monastery at a place called
Vivarium in southern Italy. It was here that he "developed a notion of the liberal arts as an aid to religious
truth," as one historian put it. Cassiodorus took the
notion of a liberal arts education and, building on the
ideas of Saint Augustine and others, transformed it into
the Christian model of education that dominated the
Western world for over a thousand years. In the process he also changed the very nature of monasticism.

As we have already seen, the early monks lived in
the desert in order to escape the temptations of city
life. As a result of Cassiodorus's success, monks also
started to preserve the best of classical learning in
their monasteries. The writing and copying of books
became one of their most important tasks. In fact, the
reason we have so many books from the ancient world
is largely down to the work of Christian monks. In their
*scriptoria* — their writing or copying rooms — they preserved the learning of the past and produced some of
the most wonderful books the world has ever seen. It
was monks who created the liberal arts as we know
them today and monks who ensured that students had
the books they needed to learn. We owe them a real
debt of gratitude.

# CHAPTER 20

# Byzantium, Justinian, and the Roman Empire

IN MANY WAYS CONSTANTINOPLE WAS A new Rome because Constantine and his successors were determined to create a capital city that was at least the equal of Rome itself. There were churches instead of temples and a **Hippodrome** for chariot racing instead of a Colosseum, but in most other ways Constantinople would have seemed much like Rome itself with its forum, public baths, and basilicas.

However, there were some obvious differences too. Constantinople was Greek-speaking for a start, which meant that the literature, learning, and, increasingly, the theology of the city was rather different from what was found in Rome. Perhaps the most obvious difference of all was Byzantine art. The Greek-speaking East, and eventually the Slavic countries it influenced (like Russia), produced art the like of which had never been seen in the West. In particular, it produced the most amazing icons.

An icon is a religious picture that is designed to lead the prayerful viewer toward the mystery it represents. So an icon of the Holy Family or an icon of the Trinity is meant to be beautiful in order to lead the person praying in front of it into a closer relationship with the Holy Family or the Trinity. This is why, in a terribly corrupted form, we have icons on our computer screens; by clicking on them we are led deeper into the particular program they represent, though the experience is never as profound as that obtained from praying before a real icon.

Visiting Greek or Russian Orthodox churches today is quite an experience for those of us brought up in the West simply because of the visual experience they provide. Every conceivable space is covered with beautiful, golden pictures of biblical and other religious scenes. The design and placing of these pictures is meant to teach and inspire. In a world where only a minority of people could read and write, the visual was hugely important. Icons are a sign of how visually literate people were in what is sometimes called Late Antiquity. We learn to read: people in Late Antiquity also learned to see.

One man who understood the power of images very well was the Emperor Justinian, who reigned from 527 to 565 and who reconquered much of the empire that had been lost to the barbarian invasions. In a series of military adventures that lasted for years, he recaptured North Africa from the Vandals, Italy from the Ostrogoths, and parts of Spain from the Visigoths. However, in doing so he all but destroyed Italy. Here again we find that the conventional story is turned on its head. It wasn't so much the barbarians who destroyed the best of the classical past, it was the Roman emperor himself.

Justinian also faced difficulties in Constantinople. In 532 some relatively small-scale disturbances got out of hand and before long a large section of the capital had been burnt to the ground by rioters. After ruthlessly suppressing the riots, Justinian realized that he had a golden opportunity to rebuild the center of the city. The centerpiece of this rebuilding program was the Church of Hagia Sophia, or the Church of Holy Wisdom. We will describe this remarkable building in the next chapter.

We can learn a huge amount about the past from buildings. They are often an untapped resource. However, there is no getting away from the fact that historians still rely primarily on written documents, which is why they spend so long considering the strengths and weaknesses of any documents they can get their hands on. In the case of Justinian, this is particularly tricky because our main source of information, a man called Procopius, wrote completely contradictory books about him. In two books he praised Justinian to the heavens but, in a third, he denounced him as a weak and terrible tyrant. Trying to get to the truth of the matter is, therefore, especially difficult.

What we can be sure about is that Justinian transformed the world in which he lived for good and for ill. He reconquered huge areas of the Western Roman Empire held by different barbarian groups and he rebuilt Constantinople in a way that proclaimed once and for all that it, rather than Rome, was now the center of the Roman world. But he made mistakes too. Though he conquered huge tracts of land, his successors weren't able to hold onto them because Justinian had overreached himself. The empire was still too big for one man to rule. His other big mistake was that he didn't take the threat from Persia seriously enough.

We haven't mentioned the Persian Empire yet but the Romans certainly knew it was there, a large and powerful empire on its eastern border. One reason the Romans were keen to have provinces like Judaea was that they acted as **buffer states** between the center of the Roman Empire and the Persian Empire, which the Romans half feared and half despised. You may have wondered why the Romans were so bothered by what went on in Jerusalem and the rest of Israel. Part of the answer is that they knew that any disorder among the Jews could give the Persians an opportunity to cause trouble in the East.

Even when Judaea was at peace the Persian Empire was more than capable of troubling the Romans. This

is what happened during Justinian's reign. As soon as
he turned his attention to Italy, North Africa, and Spain,
the Persians seized their opportunity to attack parts of
his empire. Justinian fought back but conflict between
the Persians and the Romans continued for many more
years, significantly weakening the Roman Empire and
ensuring that it shrunk again after Justinian's death
because his successors did not possess his military skill.

However, Justinian did have other successes. One
of these was in an area that you may well not have
thought much about: the law.

Justinian's reign was important because he codified
the Roman law. What does that mean? When Justinian
came to power, Roman law was incredibly complicated.
In order to make a legal decision you had to look at
not only the many laws but also at the thousands of
*responsae*, judgments that had been passed in previous
legal cases, creating what are called **precedents**. What
happened during Justinian's reign is that all this got
sorted out. Some *responsae* contradicted others. Some
areas of the law were clearer than others. By the time
his officials had finished work (it took them five years),
the empire had the Justinian code, or the *Corpus Iuris
Civilis*, made up of four books. This Justinian code was
so impressive that it became the basis of all European
law. It is, perhaps, Justinian's finest monument.

# CHAPTER 21

## *Three Great Buildings*

ONE REASON THE ROMANS STILL FASCINATE
us is that many of their buildings survive. They may
be ruins but they survive, and that is pretty remarkable given how long ago they were built. Just think
of all the thousands of houses, palaces, temples, and
other buildings that have disappeared without trace.
Just think about the number of Anglo-Saxon buildings you have seen, buildings that were built more
recently, and that we can now see only with the power
of imagination.

Two buildings stand out because of their sheer size:
the Colosseum in Rome and the Church of Hagia Sophia
in Constantinople. The Colosseum, or to give it its real
name, the Amphitheatrum Flavium, was built on the
orders of the Emperor Vespasian between AD 70 and
80. Like Hagia Sophia, it is an architectural and engi-
neering marvel, partly because it was built on marshy
ground. The builders used 300 tons of iron clamps to
hold the stone blocks together, 130,795 cubic yards of
limestone, 326,987 cubic yards of mortar and **aggregate**
to make concrete, and a million bricks. It is difficult to
work out the exact capacity of the Colosseum because it
didn't have individual seats, but it probably held about
50,000 people. These spectators sat on four different
levels (with women having to sit on the very top level).

What we can see today is extremely impressive, but
we need to remember that a lot of the Colosseum has
been lost, damaged or destroyed over the years. In its
heyday it would have been even more impressive. One
very practical part of the building that can no longer

be seen, for example, was the enormous canvas awning that protected spectators from the sun. This awning was raised and lowered by at least 1000 sailors from the Roman fleets at Misenum and Ravenna. The Church of Hagia Sophia was built almost five hundred years after the Colosseum and it is an equally impressive building. What is perhaps most striking about it is its enormous dome which stretches across almost thirty-four yards, a distance never before (and hardly ever afterward) attempted. In commissioning such a dome, Justinian was doing something new. Most early churches were modeled on basilicas, long buildings used by the Romans for government business. Justinian wanted something more like the Pantheon in Rome but bigger. And he got it. Everyone who saw Hagia Sophia was overwhelmed by the experience. Here is Procopius, who wrote about the church in *The Buildings*, his book about Justinian's building works:

> [The Church] is distinguished by indescribable beauty, excelling both in its size, and in the harmony of its measures.... The church is singularly full of light and sunshine; you would declare that the place is not lighted by the sun from without, but that the rays are produced within itself, such an abundance of light is poured into this church.... A spherical-shaped dome standing upon this circle makes it exceedingly beautiful; from the lightness of the building, it does not appear to rest upon a solid foundation, but to cover the place beneath as though it were suspended from heaven by the fabled golden chain.

It is important that we look at these buildings in context. Neither the Colosseum nor the Church of Hagia

Sophia was built as a museum. They were built to be used and they were used for very different purposes. The Colosseum was specifically built for bloody spectacles involving gladiators and wild animals, which entered the arena through an ingenious series of lifts and trap doors, while the Church of Hagia Sophia was built to the glory of God.

Gladiators are probably too well known to require much discussion here, but the animals that ended their days in the Colosseum may be less familiar. The more exotic the animal the more attractive it was to the men who paid for the spectacles. Spectators would have seen everything from elephants and lions to hippopotamuses and crocodiles. A typical show at the Colosseum would have started with wild animal hunts, followed by public executions and various warm-up acts for the gladiatorial contests, including mock fights, acrobatics, juggling, theatrical scenes, and men on stilts goading animals who struggled to reach them. Last of all came the gladiators.

We have a brief description of the events on the day the Colosseum was opened from the pen of Cassius Deo: "There was a battle between cranes," he writes, "and also between four elephants; animals both tame and wild were slain to the number of nine thousand, and women (not those of any prominence, however) took part in dispatching them. As for the men, several fought in single combat and several groups contended together in infantry and naval battles."

The Church of Hagia Sophia, by contrast, was built for worship and it is clear that not just the building but also the **liturgy** that was celebrated inside the building made a huge impact on visitors. The church was lit by thousands of candles and lamps that were hung in front of icons. Decorated curtains separated the sanctuary from the rest of the church. The clergy "burned incense, and the choirs sang hymns."

This quotation comes from the *Russian Primary Chronicle*, which describes the visit of ambassadors from Prince Vladimir of Kiev, who was trying to decide which religion to embrace. It continues:

> The emperor accompanied the Russians to the church, and placed them in a wide space, calling their attention to the beauty of the edifice, the chanting, and the offices of the archpriest and the ministry of the deacons, while he explained to them the worship of his God.

According to the ambassadors, their hosts

> ...led us to the edifices where they worship their God, and we did not know whether we were in heaven or on earth. For on earth there is no such splendor or such beauty, and we are at a loss how to describe it. We know only that God dwells there among men, and their service is fairer than the ceremonies of other nations. For we cannot forget that beauty. Every man, after tasting something sweet, is afterward unwilling to accept that which is bitter, and therefore we cannot dwell longer here.

It was the building in use—and, specifically, the liturgy—that made such an impact.

Buildings are always much more than bricks or stones. A good example is the Monastery of Saint Catherine at Sinai or, to give it its official name, the Monastery of the God-trodden Mount Sinai. Saint Catherine, whose relics were once kept in the monastery, was a fourth-century saint who is said to have been sentenced to torture on a breaking wheel before being beheaded. The Catherine wheels that are lit on Guy Fawkes night are a dim memory of the widespread devotion that used to be given to her.

The site on which the monastery was built, at the foot of Mount Horeb or Sinai, is hugely important to Jews, Christians, and Muslims. It was here that Moses saw the burning bush and here that God gave Moses the Ten Commandments. It was also in this place—in a cave on Mount Horeb—that Elijah sheltered and heard God pass by. That is why, from as early as the second century, pilgrims started to arrive. Some of these people wrote about their pilgrimages. The most remarkable of these accounts was written by a Spanish woman called Egeria whose pilgrimage took place in AD 383–384. Forget any idea you might have had about women not being able to travel or of journeys between Europe and Africa being a modern invention. Egeria traveled all the way from Spain and wrote about what she saw. This is what she said about her arrival at the monastery:

> The monks who dwelt there received us very kindly, showing us every kindness; there is also a church and a priest there. We stayed there that night, and early on the Lord's Day, together with the priest and the monks who dwelt there, we began the ascent of the mountains one by one.

A church and pilgrim's shelter seem to have been built on the site in the fourth century but the monastery that has survived to this day dates back to the Emperor Justinian's reign, though there have been many changes since then, including the building of a mosque within the monastery walls (though the monastery continues to be proudly Christian). Some of the

icons that can still be seen in the monastery date back
to Justinian's time, while many others were produced
in or for the monastery in the centuries that followed.
About half of the icons that remain from the Byzantine era can be found in the monastery, which gives
you some sense of the importance of the place. It may
be a monastery in the middle of the Egyptian desert,
but that does not mean that it is, or was, unimport-
ant. In fact, the very opposite is true. Its importance
came from the fact that it was built on the God-trodden
mountain far from the apparent centers of civilization.

   Saint Catherine's Monastery is a great building, but it
is quite different from the Colosseum and Hagia Sophia.
It was built not for show but for use, and the place
where it was built was much more important than the
building itself. More important still was what took, and
takes, place each day inside the building: the Divine
Liturgy. The building was built for the worship of God
and so it is to the liturgy that we must turn next.

# CHAPTER 22

## A History of the Liturgy

THE LITURGY, ACCORDING TO POPE BENEDICT XVI, is "the prayer of the Church, a prayer moved and guided by the Holy Spirit, a prayer in which Christ unceasingly becomes contemporary with us, enters into our lives." There can, therefore, be few topics more important for us to study.

The liturgy is not unchanging. It has developed organically. It has a history and that history goes all the way back to what happened in the Temple in Jerusalem. Since God had commanded the people of Israel to sacrifice one lamb "in the morning, and the other lamb you shall offer in the evening," the basic structure of morning and evening worship was fixed very early in the history of the people of God.

However, the Jewish people were not always able to offer sacrifices in the Temple; in the sixth century BC, for example, they were in exile in Babylon. During that time they developed synagogue services that consisted of readings from the **Torah,** psalms, and hymns. This basic structure will be very well known to you from Mass, but you may not have known that the tradition dates back over 2,500 years. When the Jewish people returned from their exile and rebuilt the Temple, they incorporated these services into their worship in the Temple. They now had worship at the third, sixth, and ninth hours of the day in addition to the morning and evening sacrifices. This was the pattern of prayer that the disciples would have been used to in Jerusalem, so it is no surprise that they continued to follow this pattern themselves after the Ascension of Jesus, as we read in the Acts of the Apostles.

However, the first Christians also introduced some crucial changes. Since Jesus had offered the sacrifice of himself on the Cross, there was no need to offer lambs as sacrifices in the Temple. Instead they celebrated the sacrifice of the Mass, as Jesus had instructed them at the Last Supper. Saint Paul explains this very carefully:

> For I received from the Lord what I also delivered to you, that the Lord Jesus on the night when he was betrayed took bread, and when he had given thanks, he broke it, and said, "This is my body which is for you. Do this in remembrance of me." In the same way also the cup, after supper, saying, "This cup is the new covenant in my blood. Do this, as often as you drink it, in remembrance of me." For as often as you eat this bread and drink the cup, you proclaim the Lord's death until he comes. (1 Cor 11:23–26)

The first Christians celebrated the Holy Eucharist in response to Jesus's instructions and example at the Last Supper. It was clearly the most important part of the liturgy. However, it was not the only part. Remembering what King David had said in Psalm 119, the first Christians also praised God "seven times a day" and, before long, this worship settled into the form of the Divine Office that we still celebrate today, largely under the influence of the early monks, the most important of whom was Saint Benedict.

The first Christians prayed in the Temple, in synagogues and in the homes of Christians. We have also seen that, during times of persecution, they worshipped in secret places, like the catacombs. However, especially after Constantine's conversion, the liturgy came to be celebrated in purpose-built churches. The early Christians took great care over the building of these churches because they knew that architecture can help shape the worship that takes place there. The way churches are built can tell you a great deal about what people believe. Jewish worshipers turned toward Jerusalem but the Christians oriented their churches toward the East and faced East themselves (*ad orientem*) during the Eucharistic celebration. The altar on which the Eucharistic Sacrifice was celebrated was also placed at the east wall. This was a change from what went before because Christians wanted to face in the symbolic direction of the New Jerusalem rather than in the direction of the earthly Jerusalem. Here is Origen, an early Christian theologian, for example, explaining the logic of their choice:

> And now we must add a few remarks on the direction in which we should face while praying. There are four cardinal points—north, south, east, and west. It should be immediately clear that the direction of the rising sun obviously indicates that we ought to pray inclining in that direction, an act which symbolizes the soul looking towards where *the true light* rises.

When Christians turned toward the Lord, toward the East, they were making a deliberate decision, a decision that would have marked them out as different from the Jewish communities among which Christianity had been born.

The words of the liturgy also gradually changed. During the first three centuries, the exact wording of the Eucharistic Prayers was not fixed, though there was a clear framework which did not greatly change. Set words for these Eucharistic Prayers then gradually

developed during the fourth century AD as it became
clear that heresies could easily creep into the liturgy
if the priest were simply left to improvise. The most
significant and influential of these Eucharistic Prayers
was the Roman Canon, which is still used today.

Early Christian worship was largely in Greek but, from
the second century onward and culminating in the fourth
century, Latin became much more widely used in the
western half of the empire, a change that occurred first
among Latin-speaking converts from North Africa. As
we shall see in a later chapter, there were plenty of other
interesting languages in and around Europe, including
Greek (as spoken in Constantinople) and Syriac (as used
in Antioch and in the Eastern churches), as well as Old
Armenian, Old Georgian, Old Ethiopian, and several other
languages that have survived in various liturgies from
around the world. However, Latin became, and remained,
the most significant language in the Western Church.

It would be easy to assume that the Latin used in the
liturgy was the language of the people but that wasn't
really the case. Many people in the Christian world spoke
other languages and those people who spoke Latin soon
began to speak less formal, more localized forms of the
language. Many languages that we are familiar with
today, including Italian, Spanish, French, and Romanian,
slowly evolved from Latin. However, the Latin of the
liturgy did not greatly change. The precise words mattered and, once they became fixed, they changed much
less quickly than the language of the people.

Gradually, from the time of Saint Gregory (who was
pope from 590 to 604), the liturgy as it was celebrated
in Rome spread across what had been the western half
of the Roman Empire. During the late eighth century,
for example, Charlemagne applied to Pope Adrian I
for a copy of the Roman Liturgy that he could use

throughout the Frankish Kingdom. There were a few other rites, such as the Ambrosian Rite at Milan, the Mozarabic Rite at Toledo, and the Byzantine Rite in Calabria and Sicily, but the Roman Rite was the most significant and widespread form during the period we are studying.

It is tempting to focus on what has changed in the Mass over the years and to forget that, essentially, the Mass has remained the same throughout the ages. One historian wrote about this a hundred years ago and what he said then is still true today:

Through all the modifications and additions that, in recent years especially, have caused our **Missal** to grow in size, among all the later **collects**, lessons and **antiphons**, the Canon stands out firm and unchanging in the midst of an ever-developing rite, the center and nucleus of the whole liturgy, stretching back with its strange and archaic formulæ through all the centuries of church history, to the days when the great Roman Caesar was lord of the world and the little community of Christians stood around their bishop while they "sang a hymn to Christ as to a God before day-break." Then the bishop lifted up his hands over the bread and wine, "gave thanks and glory to the Father of all through his Son and the Holy Ghost, and made the Eucharist." So that of all liturgical prayers in the Christian world no one is more ancient nor more venerable than the Canon of the Roman Mass.

# CHAPTER 23

# A Few of the Greats

IN AD 450 ATTILA THE HUN CAMPED OUT-
side Mantua with his army, ready to bring warfare
and destruction to Italy. In a last desperate attempt
to save themselves, the people of Rome looked for a
spokesman. The Roman emperor was far away in Constantinople and so the man who went out to meet the
terrifying barbarian leader was Pope Leo I. At a time of
political collapse, it was the popes who stepped into the
breach. Barely a hundred years after the legalization
of Christianity, the people of Rome and the people of
Italy looked to the pope rather than to the emperor for
help in their time of need.

Three years later Pope Leo was again negotiating
with barbarian invaders—this time the Vandals—but on
this occasion he could not prevent them from attacking
Rome. However, he did manage to persuade them not
to burn the city or to destroy Saint Peter's and other
churches in which terrified citizens had taken refuge.

Leo is called Saint Leo the Great not just because of his
bravery in the face of barbarian invasions but because
of all the other work he did as pope. He was a great
preacher and teacher. He made decisive interventions
in two ecumenical councils. He helped refugees and
the poor in their hour of need. When we pray, fast, and
give **alms** during Lent, it is because Saint Leo first urged
Christians to do so.

But Leo was not the only great leader to appear after
the barbarians first arrived in Italy. Another man who
changed the course of history was Saint Benedict who
was born in about AD 480 in Nursia. Sent by his parents

to study in Rome, he abandoned his studies to be closer
to God and, after living as a hermit for three years in
a place called Subiaco, he founded his first monastery
before moving to Monte Cassino and founding a monastery that remains famous to this day.

Saint Benedict is known as the founder of Western
Monasticism, not because he was the first monk in the
West but because he established a pattern that was
repeated throughout the whole of Europe and beyond
with his *Rule*, his book about how his monasteries should
be run. Slowly his monasteries, and others that took
their inspiration from his, created a new and wholly
Christian Europe.

As Pope Benedict XVI once wrote: "The Saint's work
and particularly his *Rule* were to prove heralds of an
authentic spiritual leaven which, in the course of the
centuries, far beyond the boundaries of his country
and time, changed the face of Europe following the
fall of the political unity created by the Roman Empire,
inspiring a new spiritual and cultural unity, that of
the Christian faith shared by the peoples of the Continent. This is how the reality we call 'Europe' came
into being." No wonder then that Saint Benedict is
Europe's patron saint.

One of Saint Benedict's greatest followers was
another great, Saint Gregory the Great. Gregory came
from one of the most important families in Rome and
became Prefect of the City, in effect a government official or magistrate. However, like Benedict, he turned
his back on the chance of political success and became
a monk, turning his own family home into a monastery.
After being sent to Constantinople by the pope as his
representative, he returned to Rome and, despite his
best efforts to avoid the role, was elected as pope when
the previous one died of the plague.

Gregory was a great administrator as well as a former politician, and as pope, he continued to use the skills he had learned in his earlier life. He carried out a series of tricky negotiations with the Lombards, who dominated Italy at the time, while also writing hundreds of letters to encourage bishops, abbots, and laypeople. Saint Gregory was an extremely able man but he was also a humble monk. He was the first pope to call himself the servant of the servants of God, a title still used by popes today.

There is a wonderful section in one of his sermons that gives us a vivid portrait of what his life must have been like as pope:

> When I lived in a monastic community I was able to keep my tongue from idle topics and to devote my mind almost continually to the discipline of prayer. Since taking on my shoulders the burden of pastoral care, I have been unable to keep steadily recollected because my mind is distracted by many responsibilities. I am forced to consider questions affecting churches and monasteries and often I must judge the lives and actions of individuals; at one moment I am forced to take part in certain civil affairs, next I must worry over the incursions of barbarians and fear the wolves who menace the flock entrusted to my care; now I must accept political responsibility in order to give support to those who preserve the rule of law; now I must bear patiently the villainies of brigands, and then I must confront them, yet in all charity.

After outlining his failings, Saint Gregory explained: "I do not stand on the pinnacle of achievement, I languish rather in the depths of my weakness. And yet the creator and redeemer of mankind can give me, unworthy though I be, the grace to see life whole and power to speak effectively of it. It is for love of him that I do not spare myself in preaching him."

He was indeed a great preacher and a great author too, with two of his books being of particular significance: the *Dialogues*, which are our main source of information about the life of Saint Benedict, and the *Pastoral Rule*, which describes the work of the bishop. This book was translated not only into Greek but also into Old English by none other than King Alfred the Great, which brings us to one last point about Saint Gregory: he can reasonably be regarded as great because one day he went to the market.

In his *History of the English Church and People*, Bede tells the story of the day Gregory came across some boys who were on sale in Rome's market:

> They had fair complexions, fine-cut features, and beautiful hair. Looking at them with interest, he enquired from what country and what part of the world they came. "They come from the island of Britain," he was told, "where all the people have this appearance." He then asked whether the islanders were Christians, or whether they were still ignorant heathens. "They are pagans," he was informed. "Alas!" said Gregory with a heartfelt sigh: "how sad that such bright-faced folk are still in the grasp of the Author of darkness, and that such graceful features conceal minds void of God's grace! What is the name of this race?" "They are called Angles," he was told. "That is appropriate," he said, "for they have angelic faces, and it is right that they should become joint-heirs with the angels in heaven."

According to Bede, Gregory, who was not then pope, begged the pope to send preachers to Britain and declared himself ready to go if required. He was prevented from doing so, not by the pope, but by the citizens of Rome who wanted him to stay with them. However, when he became pope, he remembered the Angles and sent a monk, the man whom we remember as Saint Augustine of Canterbury, to convert the English.

The curious thing about this story is that it is included in Bede's History almost as an afterthought. It comes in a long chapter prompted by the death of Pope Gregory, after the conversion of the English has already been described in some detail. It is, Bede tells us, a "traditional story," which perhaps sets it apart from the rest of his description of the conversion of the English, which is clearly based on solid evidence, including Pope Gregory's letters to Saint Augustine and the work of Saint Gildas.

After the Romans left in AD 410, Britain was invaded by the Angles, Saxons, and Jutes, tribes from what are now the Netherlands, Denmark, and Norway. There were already Christians in Britain during Roman times but many of them, along with the rest of the British, were pushed back into what are now Scotland, Wales, Cornwall, and Brittany. Great Britain got that name, by the way, to distinguish it from Brittany; its greatness is merely a reference to its size, though that might seem hard to believe if you live somewhere as large as the United States. England, in case you're wondering, got its name from the Angles: Angle Land. So, while Christianity survived among the Britons and among the Irish (who had never been conquered by the Romans), the rest of Britain was taken over by different Anglo-Saxon tribes, none of which were Christian.

The early history of Anglo-Saxon Britain is very controversial. Some historians argue that the Anglo-Saxons swept away any trace of Roman civilization within a few short years, while others suggest that Roman Britain faded away rather slowly. It's difficult to know for sure because the invaders were largely illiterate and so we are heavily dependent upon very limited archaeological evidence and the writings of much later authors, chief among whom is Saint Bede.

What we do know for sure is that by the time Saint Augustine arrived with his fellow monks in 597, the island was divided into separate kingdoms and that one of the most important of these was Kent. The King of Kent, called Ethelbert, was married to a Frankish princess called Bertha, "whom he had received from her parents, on condition that she should have freedom to hold and practice her faith unhindered with Bishop Liudhard, whom they had sent as her helper in the faith," as Bede puts it. As it was Bertha who had cleared the way for the arrival of the monks from Rome, we need to digress for a moment and look at how the Franks had ended up as Christians.

Like most of the barbarian tribes, the Franks had originally been pagans and *federati*, that is they had been paid by the Romans to guard parts of the empire. As the barbarians moved from being employees of the Romans to taking over Roman territory, the Franks moved into and eventually took over much of what is now France. Then, in about 500, the Frankish leader, Clovis, converted to Catholic Christianity. He was the first barbarian leader to do so. So by the time King Ethelbert of Kent took a Frankish princess as his wife, Christianity was very well established in Gaul, just as it was in Ireland and those parts of Britain that the Anglo-Saxons hadn't yet taken over.

The arrival of Saint Augustine, however, provided a new impetus. Ethelbert liked him enough to grant him a house in his capital city, Canterbury. Then, when some of his subjects accepted the new religion, an old Roman church was rebuilt and reconsecrated, which is why the Archbishop of Canterbury rather than the Bishop of London (or anywhere else) became the primate, or chief bishop, of England. When the king converted too, it was clear that Christianity had a good chance of becoming established in the whole of the island.

However, it wasn't Roman monks but Irish monks working out of Iona in Scotland who converted the north of the country. The monastery on the island of Iona had been set up by the great Irish monk Saint Columba, and it was from here that Saint Aidan traveled south at the request of King Oswald of Northumbria. Aidan became Bishop of Lindisfarne and it was from this tiny island off the north-east coast of Britain that he and his successors, the most important of whom was Saint Cuthbert, converted much of the north of the country.

The island of Lindisfarne is connected to the mainland by a narrow causeway that can be crossed only at low tide. I know this because I once crossed it when the tide wasn't that low. The car splashed through some increasingly deep water, just about getting us onto the island before nightfall. The next day we visited the local museum and saw a huge photograph of a car floating on its back downstream. The driver had attempted to cross the causeway when the tide was rising and had been swept away. If ever you visit the island of Lindisfarne read the sign before you cross! What has this got to do with history? The point is that Lindisfarne is quite isolated and yet it was from this place of isolation that Aidan, Cuthbert, and others converted the north of the country to Christianity. It was this isolated place, where seals can be seen from the shore and puffins can be seen overhead, that became a major religious and cultural center during the Anglo-Saxon era. The isolation of Lindisfarne reminds us not to jump to conclusions, historical or otherwise.

It was close to here, in a monastery in Jarrow, that Bede—the greatest writer of his age—lived and worked his whole life. A writer who seemed to be geographically adrift was actually at the center of cultural, monastic, and academic life. His work placed him right at the center of Christendom. In this respect he was an utterly typical monk. Cities can be great places but culture can survive and thrive far from the great metropolitan centers. And all of this came about because Saint Gregory the Great once visited a market in Rome!

# CHAPTER 24

## Sutton Hoo and the Struggle for Evidence

IN 1939, SHORTLY BEFORE WORLD WAR II broke out, a landowner called Mrs. Pretty persuaded a local archaeologist to dig into the largest of the mounds that were dotted across her grounds at a place called Sutton Hoo. The archaeologist, whose name was Basil Brown, wasn't too hopeful. He had already excavated three of Mrs. Pretty's mounds the previous year and had found very little because grave robbers had got there first. But this time it was a different story.

What Brown found was the pattern of a huge ship embedded in the soil together with its iron rivets. Encouraged by Mrs. Pretty to keep digging, he eventually found the burial chamber itself underneath the remains of the ship and inside were the most amazing Anglo-Saxon objects ever found in Britain and hardly equaled anywhere in the world. There was everything from drinking horns and a lyre to gold buckles, swords, a helmet, and seventh-century Frankish coins. There were also beautiful silver bowls and spoons (one with "Saulos" and one with "Paulos" engraved on them) from the region around Constantinople. But—and this was a surprise—there was no trace of a body.

Over the years, more of the mounds at Sutton Hoo were excavated and more goods were found, though none so impressive as those found in 1939 by Basil Brown. Plenty of skeletons were uncovered too but the mystery of the missing body from the largest grave of all has still not been solved.

In many ways, this mystery goes to the very heart of the difficulties historians have. If the grave robbers hadn't missed the burial chamber by chance, our picture of Anglo-Saxon England would be completely different. We would have had next to no evidence of the incredible wealth, the amazing artistry, and the international networks to which Anglo-Saxon rulers had access. But, even with the evidence from Sutton Hoo, we still have to rely on educated guesswork.

So whose ship was excavated at Sutton Hoo? It is clear from the extraordinary treasures buried with him that he must have been a king. The fact that he was buried with his ship and grave goods also tells us that he was a pagan rather than a Christian. But the two spoons confuse the picture; the names "Saulos" and "Paulos" make us think that they were baptism spoons (named after Saint Paul who was called Saul before his baptism). So we are looking for a seventh-century pagan king who owned some Christian baptism gifts.

The most obvious candidate is Redwald, King of East Anglia, who was baptized in Kent under the influence of King Ethelbert but who was persuaded by his wife and advisors to keep in with the old gods too when he returned to East Anglia. This is how Bede describes what happened: "Like the ancient Samaritans, he tried to serve both Christ and the ancient gods, and he had in the same temple an altar for the holy Sacrifice of Christ side by side with an altar on which victims were offered to devils." Redwald may well have had a pagan burial in the region of Sutton Hoo and he may well have had his baptism spoons buried with him, as well as the goods he thought he would need in the pagan afterworld.

But what happened to his body? It used to be believed that the Sutton Hoo grave belonged to someone who had been lost in battle or at sea, but now archaeologists believe that acid in the soil simply dissolved every part of the missing body, including the bones and teeth. Only the mystery remained.

There is still a good deal to be excavated at Sutton Hoo, so we hope that we will continue to learn more about Anglo-Saxon England from the site. A recent project is to build a full-size replica of the ship that was found in Mound One and then to sail it to see what can be learned about Anglo-Saxon ships and sailing. This is important because there are some basic questions for which we don't yet have answers, like how fast and how far did Anglo-Saxon ships go, how many people were needed to sail them, how much cargo could they carry, and, crucially, could they cross the North Sea?

It is an intriguing project. A very simple issue the project team faced was that they weren't entirely sure what shape the boat was. The burial mound itself put a huge amount of pressure on the boat, which must have significantly altered its shape. Another difficulty was getting hold of exactly the right materials. There were approximately 3000 rivets in the original boat, all made from bog iron, which is no longer available in those quantities. Even getting the right sort of wood is tricky. The Sutton Hoo ship seems to have been built from green wood rather than seasoned wood and so the company who built the replica had to search for exactly the same sort of wood as the Anglo-Saxons used.

We still have a problem once all these issues have been addressed. We can never get back to the working conditions and thought patterns that the original builders had. Too much practical experience has been lost. The twenty-first-century team uses computer modeling to test various different scenarios but, without the practical knowledge that the Anglo-Saxon sailors had, they cannot solve every problem. As historians, we can and must attempt to understand the past on its own terms, but the further back we travel the more we find that the past recedes in front of us, like a distant horizon we can never quite reach.

# CHAPTER 25

## *What's in a Name?*

IMAGINE A VALLEY WHERE WILD SAFFRON grows. Picture in your mind's eye a pear-tree wood. Think about a village on a small hill. What do you see? You see three urban areas in London as they might have been in Anglo-Saxon times: Croydon, Purley, and Clapham. How do we know? Because the names themselves tell us so.

We are all familiar with the fact that names, our names, mean something, but it's easy to forget that place names mean something too, and that these names can be a very rich source of information for historians. The very fact that a place has an Anglo-Saxon rather than an Old Norse (i.e., Viking) or British name can be very useful to us. It tells us who once lived there. But it's not just the languages that matter; it's the names themselves as well. So let's look at some specific examples.

Croydon gets its name from "croh," the Old English word for saffron (which also gives us the word "crocus" in Modern English) and "denu," the Old English word for a valley (which should not be confused with the Old English "dun" which means "hill" and which is found in place names like Coulsdon and Selsdon). Purley, by contrast, derives its name from "pirige," the Old English word for a pear-tree, and "leah," the Old English word for a forest, wood, or clearing. And Clapham probably comes from "cloppa," an Old English word for a small hill, and "ham," the Old English word for a village.

I was born and bred on the edge of Frindsbury and Strood in Kent. "Strōd" is an Old English word for marshy land overgrown with brushwood, while Frindsbury comes from an Old English word meaning *Freond's fortification. That asterisk, by the way, means that we have no written record of the name Freond, but that we are pretty certain it existed from linguistic evidence. It's all pretty complicated stuff so I won't go into the details here, but if you want to learn more and find out about *The Hobbit* and *The Lord of the Rings* at the same time, I can heartily recommend Tom Shippey's *The Road to Middle-Earth*.

But back to place names. You might be familiar with many places that have "Chester" as part of their name. The reason "Chester" appears in so many place names is because "ceaster" was an Old English word meaning a city, an old fortification, or (crucially) a Roman site. So Rochester, where I went to school, probably means a Roman town called *Hrofi.

Other Old English words may be less familiar. When I was a child, I broke my arm playing football at a place called Hoo. It's a great name but I had no idea then that it came from the Old English word for a heel or a sharply projecting piece of ground: "hōh."

Tracking down these original meanings is great fun but sometimes we have to accept that we just don't know where names came from. Even really important places like London. Its name may be a very corrupt version of the name of a British river but no one is quite sure. Fortunately we are on safer ground with different parts of London, like Hammersmith (whose meaning is obvious) and Westminster (which simply means the west monastery).

Westminster and Hammersmith may be relatively easy to explain but sometimes place names can reveal unexpected stories. Elterwater in the English Lake District, for example, means "Swan Lake." I used to live

near another place in the Lake District called Sunbrick.
Have a think about how it might have got that name.
Almost certainly, you won't have guessed that "Sun" is
a corruption of "svin" or "swine," ("pig" in other words)
and that "Brick" comes from the Old Norse "brekka"
meaning a slope. So Sunbrick has nothing to do with
the sun or bricks, but was once a place where pigs for-
aged on a slope, which also tells us that Sunbrick must
once have been wooded (which, alas, it is no longer)
because that is how the Vikings farmed their pigs.

Some of the words we find in place names are still in
use today. The Old English word for forest, for example, was "wald," but in different parts of Britain there
were different spellings and pronunciations, so in Kent
and Wessex "wald" became "weald," giving us names
with which British readers might still be familiar,
like the Weald of Kent. It also lives on in many place
names; Woldingham, for instance, means "village of
the forest people."

But what did all these places actually look like? As
we have very little written or archaeological evidence,
we have to be inventive. When historians want to learn
about prehistory, they sometimes look at pollen evidence from peat bogs and lakes in order to build up a
picture of the vegetation in a particular area, but this
is less accurate for more recent times. We know from
place names and other written evidence that some animals that are now extinct in Britain, like the beaver, the
wolf, and the crane, may once have lived in Anglo-Saxon
England, but it's difficult to be certain about how many
there were and where exactly they lived.

In fact, it is sometimes easier to say what *wouldn't*
have been seen in Anglo-Saxon Britain. The rabbit, for
example, was only introduced into the country in the
twelfth century and grey squirrels appeared centuries

later. Much the same is true of some very familiar trees and plants, like the sycamore and rosebay willowherb, which were probably introduced as late as the sixteenth century.

The picture of Anglo-Saxon England that we are often given in books and films is of a widely wooded country, but in fact the evidence suggests otherwise. If we look at a combination of archaeological evidence, legal documents known as charters, and, especially, the Domesday Book drawn up by the Norman invaders in the eleventh century, we see that only a tiny percentage of the country was covered in woodland.

But, as so often happens when studying the past, we have to accept a certain amount of ignorance while always striving to fill in the historical gaps where we can. Anglo-Saxon England may be easy to imagine but it is not always easy to tell whether our historical imagination is giving us an accurate picture of the past.

# CHAPTER 26
## A Taste of the Past

**WHAT DID PEOPLE EAT AND DRINK IN THE** past? It's a daft question because it depended entirely on when and where you lived and who you were.

So where do we look for evidence? Let's start with literature. Take this example from *The Satyricon* written possibly in the first century AD:

> A tray followed them on which was set a boar of great size with a liberty-cap above him, while there hung from his tusks two little palm-leaf baskets, one full of nut-shaped dates, and the other full of Theban dates. All around were little suckling pigs made of pastry, signifying that the boar was supposed to represent a sow. These were intended for keepsakes to carry away... a big fellow with a beard, wearing leggings and with a light cloak on his shoulders, slashed the side of the boar vigorously with a drawn hunting-knife, till out of the gash live thrushes flew forth. Bird-catchers were at hand with long rods, and they caught the birds very quickly as they were fluttering around the dining-room. Trimalchio ordered a bird to be given to each guest.

If we imagine that this was a typical Roman meal we would be entirely wrong. In fact, the whole point of this humorous passage is to mock the vulgar Trimalchio who used his dinner party as an occasion to show off. What we have here is an exaggeration of reality.

So what was the reality? That very much depended on when and where you lived and what job you had.

Take wine, for instance. The Greeks used to water down their wine while the Romans tended to prefer it neat. So far, so straightforward. Mead (which was made by fermenting diluted honey) and beer were brewed in northern Europe and were drunk by the Romans in Germany and Britain.

But grapes were grown in Britain too. There were vineyards in Britain in Roman times and Bede, right at the start of his *History of the English Church and People*, mentions vines growing in his day. The Romans on the European continent, by contrast, sometimes had to make do with *posca*, vinegar-with-water. It is entirely possible that there were Britons drinking wine made in Britain while Roman soldiers were drinking watered down vinegar in Italy (though it's also true that exactly the opposite must have happened as well).

We mustn't jump to easy conclusions when studying the past, nor should we make the mistake of focusing on apparently grotesque customs. The reason we home in on Romans who ate dormice is because we like to distance ourselves from the past. If the past was horrible then we don't need to think too carefully about adjusting the way we do things today. To take another example, let's think about the eating of brains. We know from books like *De Cibis* written in Constantinople in about the seventh century that everything from pigs' snouts to buffalo to various brains were eaten in the city. On the face of it, this evidence suggests that people in the past were completely unlike us. However, if we probe more deeply we discover that most people in Constantinople didn't eat buffalo or brains because they knew that "buffalo is cold, indigestible, heavy, not nourishing, and altogether unhealthy: those who eat it frequently develop leprosy, elephantiasis, diseases of black bile and other disgusting illnesses" while "brain creates heaviness in the stomach and tends to be emetic [in other words, it made you vomit]: it should be eaten with pepper or mustard." If we focus on foods we would find unpalatable we'll never really understand the taste of the past.

So how do we find out what foods used to be eaten? Written sources can be very helpful—we have everything from travelers' accounts to recipe books—but archaeology really comes into its own where food is concerned, simply because archaeologists are great at digging up drains, rubbish dumps, and what are quaintly referred to as latrines. So let's have a look at the sewers in Herculaneum.

The first people to excavate Herculaneum in earnest threw away sacks full of Roman food because they didn't consider it important. Recent archaeologists have gone to the other extreme, examining the contents of the city's drains in minute detail. So far 774 bags of organic matter have been collected from one drain alone, revealing a hoard of chicken eggs, olive pips, and 2,682 fish bones.

Fish bones are very interesting. Especially their ear bones. Why would anyone be interested in a fish's ear bones (or otoliths, to use the technical term)? The answer is because these bones help us identify the type and age of fish. Ear bones can tell us which fish the people of Herculaneum ate, which was everything from warty crabs to cuttlefish to oysters and much much more besides. Their diet was incredibly rich.

Another fascinating discovery just down the coast in Pompeii was a jar of pure garum. Or, possibly, *kosher* garum. Garum, or fish sauce, was hugely popular in the Roman world but since it was made from lots of different fish it wasn't a product Jews were necessarily able to use. This was because Jews were not allowed to eat shellfish. Kosher fish sauce would have been shellfish-free and was advertised as such.

We have come a long way from live thrushes inside pigs but it simply goes to show where the study of an apparently unpromising aspect of the past can lead you. A jar of fish sauce inscribed with just two words is the only evidence we have of a possible Jewish community in Pompeii.

Garum shows us the pastness of the past. While we use salt to flavor our food, the Romans used fish sauce. A Roman cookbook known as *Apicius* lists hundreds of recipes that require fish sauce but only three that require salt. In other words, fashions change. In fact, even fish sauce was to have its day. By the tenth century when Liutprand, the Bishop of Cremona, visited Constantinople it had been all but forgotten in Italy. In fact Liutprand seems to have come across garum for the first time in Constantinople. He was not impressed.

"This dinner was quite nasty," he wrote, "and unspeakable, drunkenly awash with oil and drenched with another very unpleasant liquid made from fish." What had once been considered essential in Italy had now, a few short centuries later, been so forgotten that it could be regarded as unspeakably nasty.

We can't just dip into the past because history is not a buffet or, even worse, a pick 'n' mix sweet counter. What studying food tells us is that nothing is settled forever. Tastes change. Societies change. Fashions change. And there's no better way of seeing the importance of these changes than by looking at the history of the cucumber.

It is possible to have a history of anything: the history of food; the history of the cucumber; even the history of history. In fact, there is a special word for the history of history: historiography.

Why would we want a history of history? One reason is that it helps us understand how and why interpretations of the past change. So let's have a look at the history of the history of the cucumber. Or if that's too much of a mouthful, let's look at the historiography of the cucumber.

The cucumber (or *Cucumis sativus*, to give it its scientific name) originated in India and was taken to China about two thousand years ago. Historians used to think that the cucumber also came West and that it was known and eaten by the ancient Egyptians, Greeks, Romans, and Jews. That view has now changed.

The current consensus of opinion is that cucumbers reached what we now call Iran, Iraq, and Turkey by the sixth or seventh century AD, Spain by the ninth century, and Italy by the eleventh century. So why have historians changed their minds?

One reason is that cucumbers look very much like certain melons (especially the so-called snake melon or snake cucumber). Historians used to point to Egyptian and Roman wall paintings as evidence of cucumbers in those places but it is now thought that these pictures depict melons instead. To understand why they made this mistake we need to come to grips with science. Cucumbers flourish in relatively low temperatures, such as you get in northern Europe and in the hills of northern India. Melons grow much more successfully in warmer climates. Perhaps it's no surprise then that historians from northern Europe tended to forget about melons when looking at Roman and Egyptian pictures.

Maybe they should have turned to archaeology instead. The problem for archaeologists is that the remains of cucumbers very rarely survive (because they are moist and soft) and so are hardly ever found during archaeological digs. Their seeds may survive but as it is virtually impossible to distinguish them from melon seeds that isn't much help.

So, if archaeology can't help us, what about the written evidence? Words that might represent the cucumber appear in plenty of documents (including the Old Testament) but the problem is one of translation. What exactly did the Greeks mean by *sikyos*, or the Romans by *cucumis*? What, for that matter, does the Hebrew word *qishut* mean? Let's have a look at different translations of the Book of Numbers, Chapter 11, verse 5.

*We remember the fish, which we did eat in Egypt freely; the cucumbers, and the melons, and the leeks, and the onions, and the garlick.* (King James Version)

*We remember the fish we ate in Egypt for nothing, the cucumbers, the melons, the leeks, the onions, and the garlic.* (Revised Standard Version)

*Think of the fish we used to eat free in Egypt, the cucumbers, melons, leeks, onions and garlic!* (Jerusalem Bible)

So far, the evidence seems pretty clear. But what about this translation from the fourteenth century that doesn't mention cucumbers at all?

*We think upon the fish that we ate in Egypt freely; gourds, and melons, and leeks, and onions, and garlic come into our mind.* (Wycliffe Bible)

Translation can be a tricky business. We cannot assume that when a translator used a word like "cucumber" he was describing what the original author had in mind. But this doesn't mean we have to throw up our hands and ignore the problem. What historians have done is look very closely at the different words that were used to describe cucumbers and melons over a period of time. This information, alongside the evidence from pictures and archaeology, suggests that the cucumber eventually arrived in Europe by two different routes, the first from Persia into eastern and northern Europe by land and the second from Persia or India into Spain by sea.

Why does any of this matter? What conclusions can we draw from the historiography of the cucumber?

Firstly we can say that globalization is not a new phenomenon. Goods and products traveled the world two thousand years ago (and before that too).

Secondly, studying the cucumber reminds us that we need to look at a wide range of evidence if we are to understand the past: in this case, written evidence, archaeological evidence, scientific evidence, and the evidence of pictures.

Thirdly, the history of the cucumber tells us that historical judgments change, which is one reason the past is so fascinating.

And, lastly, the history of the cucumber reminds us that nothing is off limits for the historian. Everything has a history. Even the food on your plate.

# CHAPTER 27

## *The Rise of Islam*

IF YOU WANT TO KNOW WHY HISTORY MAT-
ters and if you want to know why history can be controversial, you need look no further than the early days
of Islam. Islam, Christianity, and Judaism are all historical religions; their truth claims are based on historical
events. We need, therefore, to tread very gently and
to examine our sources very carefully when examining
the origins of each of these religions.

So let's start with the undisputed facts. We know
that a merchant from Mecca called Muhammad started
preaching to the people of Mecca in the early seventh
century. However, his message was opposed in the
city so he was forced to move to Medina in 622 before
returning to Mecca with an army shortly before his
death in 632. After his death his followers had a run of
spectacular military successes. They conquered Syria
and Egypt by 643, Iraq and most of Iran by 660, and
North Africa and most of Spain by 713.

That much we know for certain: most other details
are disputed. Our main historical source is, of course,
the Qur'an, the book which Muhammad claimed to have
received by revelation over a series of years from the
angel Gabriel (or Jibril). Understandably, different historians take very different positions on when it was
written and when it was compiled into one book, quite
apart from whether it represents an authentic revelation from God. The evidence is hotly disputed because
it makes such a difference to people today. The nature
of the Qur'an is not simply a historical question.

If we are to understand how Islam became a political

and religious force to be reckoned with, we need to understand something of the nature of Islam itself. Islam, which means "submission" to God, is very much a religion of the book. In fact, strictly speaking, it is the only religion of the book. Jews and Christians possess inspired Scriptures but these holy books are holy because they speak of the actions of God in history, the Jewish Torah describing the saving actions of the God of Israel and the Christian Bible describing, above all, the love of God as revealed in the death and Resurrection of Jesus Christ, the Word of God. As Pope Benedict XVI once wrote, "While in the Church we greatly venerate the sacred Scriptures, the Christian faith is not a 'religion of the book': Christianity is the 'religion of the word of God,' not of 'a written and mute word, but of the incarnate and living Word.'"

Like Christianity and Judaism, Islam is a monotheistic religion but the Qur'an marks it out as quite different from the monotheistic religions that came before it. Muslims revere the Old Testament prophets and Jesus, whom they regard as a prophet, but they see Muhammad as the last and greatest of the prophets and the Qur'an as the definitive revelation of God.

Islam was a religion that drew no distinction between religious and political authorities. Muhammad's aim was to set up a new community with its own government, laws, and institutions. This is quite different from what we find in Christianity. Even when the emperor became more closely involved in religious affairs than we would feel comfortable with or when the pope took more political power than was good for him, it was clear that Church and State were different. In Islam religion and politics were intertwined, which is why, when Muhammad died, Abu Bakr took over as the Caliph, the political and religious leader of all Muslims.

Islam split into two distinctive groups in its early days: Sunnis and Shi'as. It is easy for Christians to assume that Sunnis and Shi'as are the Islamic equivalent of Catholics and Protestants, but the comparison is not a helpful one. The division came about because of the importance of the Caliph. The fourth Caliph, Ali, was Muhammad's son-in-law and when he was killed power passed not to his son but to a rival Caliph. Eventually rivalry led to fighting and a division between those who claimed that the Caliph should come from Ali's family (the Shi'as) and those who did not (the Sunnis). Since the Shi'as then rejected the first three Caliphs, Abu Bakr, Omar, and Othman (believing that Ali should have gained the position immediately after the death of Muhammad), it became impossible to **reconcile** the two groups. So, although there are now some differences of belief between Sunnis and Shi'as (as well as differences of belief within these two groups), it was not **doctrinal** differences as such that originally divided them.

It was at this time, about 661, that the capital of the Caliphate—the area ruled by Muslims—shifted from Medina to Damascus in modern-day Syria. It was during these years when the Caliphs were drawn from the Umayyad dynasty, an important family from Mecca, that the Great Mosque of Damascus and the Dome of the Rock at Jerusalem were built.

The Umayyads were eventually toppled from power in 750 by the Abbasid family mainly because they failed to keep their non-Arab subjects happy. The Abbasid family then moved the center of the Islamic empire to Baghdad. Islam's center of gravity shifting eastward had important consequences for later religious and political history. It was here in Baghdad that Islam flourished and here that great centers of learning were set up.

It was not just Muslims who lived and worked in Baghdad. As far as they could, the Muslim conquerors left local leaders in control and set up **garrison towns** for Islamic soldiers. This had two main effects: firstly, Muslims and non-Muslims often lived very separate lives (though this changed over time); secondly, such an arrangement enabled the conquering armies to move swiftly on to other regions. According to laws called the *dhimma*, Christians and Jews were allowed to practice their religion and be governed by their own laws in Muslim-controlled areas, though they did have to pay much higher taxes. It was therefore in the interest of Muslims not to convert Christians and Jews (because they wouldn't receive as much tax revenue if they did) and it was in non-Muslims best financial interests to convert, which, over time, many did.

Even so, Christians and Muslims tended to show very little interest in each other's religion. The Qur'an wasn't translated into Latin until the twelfth century, for example. This is perhaps not as surprising as it seems at first. In the same way that Christians see the New Testament as, in some sense, completing the Hebrew Bible (the Old Testament), Muslims see the Qur'an as the true Scripture, replacing the disfigured or incomplete version preserved by Christians and Jews. What this meant in practice was that Muslims and Christians tended to ignore each other's scriptures.

However, there were exceptions to this general rule and one of those exceptions was Yuhanna ibn Mansur ibn Sarjun. I am working here on the assumption that well over ninety-nine percent of you will never have heard of Yuhanna ibn Mansur ibn Sarjun. There is no reason why you should have done, apart from the fact that he is a tremendously important figure in the history of Christian culture and a Doctor of the Church, a Doctor not in the sense of a physician, but a teacher. As the Church has recognized only thirty-six men and women as Doctors, great teachers of the whole Church, during its two thousand years of history, it is certainly worth finding out about him.

Yuhanna ibn Mansur ibn Sarjun came from a distinguished Arab Christian family. His grandfather, Mansur, lived and worked in Damascus for the Roman Emperor Heraclius. His father, Sergius, also worked for the government in Damascus but by this time the government had become a Muslim one. Yuhanna followed in his father's footsteps and also worked for the Umayyad caliphate in Damascus, until in midlife he took a new name, John, and a new job: he became a monk in the monastery of Saint Saba between Jerusalem and the Dead Sea. It is as John of Damascus or John Damascene that he is better known today.

John of Damascus is an important figure in history because he was the first Christian theologian to address the challenge presented by the arrival and military success of Islam. He was a speaker of Arabic, a former civil servant of the highest rank, and had also clearly read at least some of the Qur'an, which is quite significant, as the Muslims' holy book hadn't yet been translated into Latin. He was, therefore, in a position to write with some authority about this new religion as he did in two books, a *Dialogue between a Saracen and a Christian* and *On Heresies*.

Although John was very critical indeed of Islam, he remained a monk in Muslim-held territory. One reason for this may well have been that he was also strongly opposed to iconoclasm, the movement that was sweeping through the Roman Empire at this time. At various points between 726 and 843, the emperors in Constantinople ordered that all religious images, including icons, statues and stained glass windows, had to be destroyed because they were distracting the faithful from the worship of God. There is a striking similarity between this movement and Islamic attitudes toward images, though whether there was any direct link between the two is still an open question for historians. John of Damascus took the same position as the pope and the Western Church, seeing icons and other religious images as aids to worship. According to John of Damascus, icons lead worshippers away from themselves and toward God in much the same way that relics take Christians from the physical to the spiritual.

The late sixth and seventh centuries were unexpectedly rich times for the Church in Syria with several popes during these years being born in the region. This meant that John of Damascus was not cut off from the Christian mainstream, as you might have expected from a monk living in an area under Muslim control, well away from both Rome and Constantinople. We need to avoid geographical bias quite as much as historical bias when looking at the past. John of Damascus was able to write with great authority about a range of theological subjects and to become an influential figure within the Church as a whole from his monastery in a Muslim-controlled area. Islam may have swept away the old certainties but the Church's work went on.

# CHAPTER 28
## Christian and Muslim Spain

SPAIN HAS A PARTICULARLY INTERESTING religious history. We know from the Bible that Saint Paul wanted to travel there on one of his missionary journeys. We also know that the country had quite a lot of Jewish communities from the first century onward, which may have been one of the reasons why Saint Paul considered going there to preach. However, it seems to have been Saint James who brought the gospel to the country, which explains why the cathedral at Santiago de Compostela where he was buried became one of the great pilgrimage sites of later centuries.

Spain was an important part of the Roman Empire, with the emperors Trajan and Theodosius being born in the country. It was then conquered by the Visigoths who, like most of the barbarian tribes, were Arians at first but later converted to Catholicism. The Visigoths created an enormous kingdom that stretched from the Spanish peninsula into Gaul. Several important writers then emerged from the country, including Saint Isidore, who was Bishop of Seville. Isidore wrote one of the great books of the seventh century, the *Etymologies*, a sort of cross between an encyclopedia and a dictionary, containing information on everything from grammar to animals, from games to angels.

However, from the late seventh century, Spain started to come under attack from Berber tribesmen from North Africa. These tribesmen had mostly converted to Islam and were attracted by the wealth and comparatively lush countryside they found across what later became known as the Straits of Gibraltar. In 712, they defeated the Visigothic king in battle, conquered Toledo, the capital city, and soon had control of most of the country. Since the Visigothic kingdom stretched into what we now call France, the religious geography of the continent was changed almost overnight. Very few written documents survive from the time but we have an intriguing treaty made between Abd al-Aziz and Theodemir, a local leader in south-east Spain, in 713. In the treaty Theodemir submitted to Abd al-Aziz and in return was allowed to keep his position, while his people were promised safety and the right to continue to practice their Christian faith. Theodemir also had to promise not to help deserters or his conquerors' enemies as well as to pay an annual poll tax. It may well be that this approach was copied across the country, which would help to explain the Berbers' phenomenal success.

Some of the Muslims who conquered Spain didn't want to stop there. Some of them pushed into France, setting up a new capital at Narbonne. From there they were able to take over most of Aquitaine and Bordeaux. When Abdul al-Rahman, emir of Córdoba, attempted to conquer more of France, Odo of Aquitaine turned to a man called Charles Martel for help. Charles Martel was, in effect, the ruler of the Frankish kingdoms. Sensing an opportunity to gain control of Aquitaine and fearing the advance of Abdul al-Rahman, he came to Odo's help and won a crucial battle at Tours in 732. Having swept all before him, Abdul al-Rahman became complacent and was unprepared for Charles Martel's disciplined troops, who defeated the Muslim cavalry and killed Abdul al-Rahman himself. The Muslim forces were forced back into Spain and Charles Martel, who became a hero across Christendom, took control of most of what we now call France.

The Frankish kingdom remained Christian but Spain changed dramatically as a result of the Berber Muslim conquest. For a start, there was a huge influx of Arab and Berber warriors, many of whom brought wives, children, and slaves with them. It is difficult to know how many people moved to Spain, but it was at least 150,000 and quite possibly a much higher number. With Islam now the dominant religion, the native population of what is often called **al-Andalus** began to take on the religion of their political masters. By 800 about eight percent of the local population had become Muslims, by 900 the figure was about twenty-five percent, by 950 it was fifty percent, and by 1000 it was seventy-five percent, with the percentage staying fairly stable after that.

There are several interesting points to note here. As we have already seen, conversions to Islam are not surprising given the fact that non-Muslims paid much higher taxes than Muslims did, but we shouldn't forget another reason for conversion: marriage. When Christians married into Muslim families, the children of that marriage were considered as Muslims under Islamic law and were forbidden to convert on pain of death, even if their mother or father remained a Christian.

The longer Islam was the dominant force in the country the more attractive it became to those people who wanted to get on in society. However, it was perfectly possible to be a Christian or a Jew in Muslim Spain and to live a comfortable life, as long as you kept your head down and didn't antagonize the religious and political authorities (who were, of course, the same people). The Church survived in Spain and Christians, including Christian bishops, served the new government at the highest levels.

Peace came at a cost though, as the events of 851 showed. In that year a man called Isaac, who came from a Christian family in Córdoba, was executed. As a well-educated man and a fluent Arabic speaker, he had worked for the government before deciding to resign his position and become a monk in a place called Tábanos. Three years later he returned to Córdoba, presented himself to the *qadi*, the officer responsible for religious observance, and announced that he wanted to become a Muslim. However, as soon as the *qadi* started to explain Islam, Isaac denounced Muhammad and tried to convert the *qadi* to Christianity. After being imprisoned, Isaac still refused to recant and was executed.

So what do we make of his death? The first point to make is that he was not alone. Forty-seven other Christians were killed between 850 and 859. Some of them denounced Muhammad as a magician, an adulterer, and a liar and said that his followers would go to hell. Some were monks, others were priests, laymen, or laywomen. Some had Muslim siblings and parents. Some, like Isaac, had worked for the Islamic government. When they refused to recant, they were publicly decapitated with a sword and then either burnt, thrown into the river, displayed on hooks or simply left in the streets to rot.

The deaths divided the Christian community in Córdoba, especially when the government began closing monasteries, arresting priests, raising Christian taxes, and sacking Christians from government service. Some Christians saw those who had been killed as martyrs for the faith but others saw them as troublemakers who had unnecessarily brought about their own deaths by refusing to keep quiet about their beliefs and by provoking the authorities. Those Christians who stayed in the country during the difficult years that followed tended not to antagonize the authorities. Martyrdoms came to an end.

However, the country was far from peaceful. Throughout the ninth and tenth centuries, Islamic armies fought not only within Spain itself but also increasingly against the principalities of North Africa. The fall of the Umayyads in distant Damascus also had an impact in Spain, with a member of the family setting up the Caliphate of Córdoba in opposition to the Abbasids, which meant that there was a lot of internal strife as well as continued fighting against northern and western Spain, some of which had remained Christian and was outside Muslim control. And if that wasn't enough to keep the armies busy, a new empire and potential threat had emerged in an unlikely place, north-western Europe.

# CHAPTER 29

## Charlemagne and Alcuin

ON CHRISTMAS DAY IN 800 THE POPE crowned the new emperor, the first emperor of the Western Roman Empire for over three hundred years. The new emperor came not from Rome or even from Constantinople but from Aachen in a north-western corner of Europe, and his name was Charlemagne, or Charles the Great, King of the Franks.

Charlemagne came from a family that had only limited political power. His ancestors were powerful officials in Merovingian France. At first they served the Frankish kings but eventually they grew more powerful and wanted to become kings in their own right. The most well-known of these men was Charles Martel, Charlemagne's grandfather, whose son, Pepin (or Pippin), succeeded him. Pepin was so keen to develop his power base that he persuaded Pope Stephen to cross the Alps and crown him. Pope Stephen needed help in keeping the Lombards out of Rome and he also needed an ally against the religious authorities in Constantinople who were going through a phase of iconoclasm, so he traveled north to meet Pepin, passing within a few miles of Muslim-held territory. He was the first pope ever to travel north of the Alps.

When he became king after Pepin died, Charlemagne set about extending his kingdom. His father and grandfather had already established control in France, winning back territory from the Muslims who had taken over the Visigothic kingdom in Spain and France, but Charlemagne went further by defeating the Lombards in Italy, the Avars in what is now Hungary, and the Bavarians and Saxons. He also fought in Spain and it was one of these battles that provided the inspiration for *The Song of Roland*, one of the greatest works of literature of its age. Charlemagne was now much more than the king of the Franks and so having himself crowned emperor was a logical next step.

The empire over which he ruled was in many ways quite different from the Roman Empire. Ever since Pope Stephen had crossed the Alps, it had been clear that the center of political power in Europe had shifted from south to north. Charlemagne made no attempt to move his capital from Aachen but he certainly saw himself as a Christian emperor and his empire as a Holy Roman Empire. Not only was he crowned by the pope in Rome, something Constantine would never have contemplated, but he also set about reviving Christian learning and culture.

It is a curious irony that it was the soldier Charlemagne who could hardly read or write who brought about this great revival of learning. But Charlemagne—who slept with a copy of Saint Augustine's *City of God* by his bedside—realized the value of education. There is a moving passage in the *Life of Charlemagne* written by his friend Einhard that makes this clear:

He paid the greatest attention to the liberal arts; and he had great respect for men who taught them. When he was learning the rules of grammar he received tuition from Peter the Deacon of Pisa, who by then was an old man, but for all the other subjects he was taught by Alcuin, surnamed Albinus, another Deacon, a man of the Saxon race who came from Britain and was the most learned man anywhere to be found. Under him the Emperor spent much time and effort in studying rhetoric,

dialectic and especially astrology. He applied himself to mathematics and traced the course of the
stars with great attention and care. He also tried
to learn to write. With this object in view he used
to keep writing-tablets and notebooks under the
pillows on his bed, so that he could try his hand
at forming letters during his leisure moments; but,
although he tried very hard, he had begun too late
in life and he made little progress.

This is a very human moment, which brings the
greatest man of his age down to our level. However,
his struggles with writing did not hold him back. His
aim was nothing less, as he put it himself, than "to
restore with diligent zeal the workshops of knowledge,
which, through the negligence of our ancestors, have
been well-nigh deserted. We invite others by our own
example as much as lies within our power to learn to
practice the liberal arts."

That is why he brought the greatest scholars of his
day right into the heart of his government. Classical
learning and the liberal arts were not optional extras
for students who had time on their hands, but instead
were seen as essential if Charlemagne's empire was to
survive and prosper. However, classical learning did
not exist in a void. Charlemagne was also determined to
restore reverence to the liturgy. According to Einhard,
"He went to church morning and evening with great
regularity, and also for early-morning Mass, and the
late-night hours. He took the greatest pains to ensure
that all church ceremonies were performed with the
utmost dignity."

Charlemagne's reform covered everything from
the liturgy to spelling, from handwriting to rhetoric,
from mathematics to education itself. In fact the reason

we still have the works of Livy and Tacitus is that they were salvaged from places like Ravenna, Monte Cassino, and Rome and then copied during the **Carolingian Renaissance**. Charlemagne could be a ruthless and bloodthirsty soldier but he did more than anyone else from 500–1000 to spread Christian knowledge and culture and, as we shall see in a later chapter, his ideas and example didn't die with him.

Charlemagne's ambitious program of spiritual, cultural, and intellectual renewal was a great international movement that drew on the work of the best scholars in Europe at the time. And, as it happened, the greatest scholar of them all came from England: Alcuin of York. Despite being cut off from classical civilization for many years after the Romans left Britain, and despite being conquered by the Anglo-Saxons who were illiterate at first, the people of Britain soon found themselves at the center of Europe's intellectual life.

As we have already seen, Saint Bede, who lived his whole life in an apparently remote monastery in Northumbria, was the greatest scholar of his age but he was not a solitary genius. One reason for this is that Jarrow was not actually cut off from the rest of Christian civilization. The founder of Bede's monastery, Benedict Biscop, made five visits to Rome during his life, which is more than I have managed even with the advantages of planes, trains, and cars. The English, in other words, were very much part of the Christian world centered on Rome.

Northumbria was a center of Christian culture then, with some of the most beautiful books in Europe at that time being created in the north-east of England, including the Lindisfarne Gospels, which are one of the British Museum's most prized possessions, and the Codex Amiatinus, the first complete version of the Vulgate to have survived. When the pope asked a man called Wynfrith, a contemporary of Bede's, to lead a missionary expedition to Germany, he took a collection of books as well as a group of well-educated men and women with him. The English were well-educated and keen to spread their Christian education to others. What is striking about Wynfrith's missionary journey is that it wasn't an exclusively English endeavor. It was the pope in Rome who asked Wynfrith, or Boniface as he was renamed, to go, but he also had the active support of the Frankish leader, Charles Martel.

Years later Boniface was attacked by pirates in what is now the Netherlands. He tried to defend himself with one of his books but he was still killed. If you go to Fulda Cathedral in Germany today, you can see amazing relics from that time: the sliced-up bones of Boniface and his fellow Anglo-Saxon missionaries, and the scarred and gashed eighth-century manuscript that he used as a shield.

But let's return to Alcuin, who was educated at the school Bede established and who lived from something like 740 to 804. Having come to Charlemagne's attention while running York Minster's school and library, he was recruited to run the palace school at Aachen. There he joined a group of scholars from all round Europe: Theodulph of Orleans who was probably a Visigoth, Paul the Deacon who was probably a Lombard, and Einhard who was a Frank.

One of the tasks Alcuin set himself when he came to Aachen was to make math fun, so he asked his students questions like these:

1. A snail is invited to supper by a swallow who lives a league away, but the snail can travel only an inch a day. How long does it take him to get there (if a league is 7,500 feet and a foot is twelve inches)?

2. A man had to take a wolf, a goat, and some cabbages across a river in a small boat that could carry only the man and one object at a time. How did the man get all his goods safely across the river without either the goat or the cabbages being eaten? The answers to these questions can be found at the bottom of this page.*

Charlemagne's reforms and Alcuin's work continued to be highly influential long after their deaths but, before we look at the impact they had in Britain and elsewhere, we need to look at a rather unusual present Charlemagne received a year or so after his coronation as emperor.

---

* Solutions:
1. 246 years and 210 days.
2. Take the goat across, leaving the wolf and the cabbages behind. Then return and take the wolf across. Having left the wolf on the other side, take the goat back over. Having left the goat behind, take the cabbages across. Then row across once more, pick up the goat, and take it to the far side.

## CHAPTER 30

# An Elephant at the Court of Charlemagne

IN 802 CHARLEMAGNE RECEIVED A REMARK-
able present. It came all the way from Baghdad and
was a gift from the Caliph of Baghdad, Harun al-Rashid,
who was the most powerful Islamic ruler in the world
at that time and who was later immortalized in literature in *The Thousand and One Nights.* Harun al-Rashid's
present to Charlemagne was an elephant.

The elephant's name was Abul-Abbas and we're not
sure how he got to Baghdad in the first place (because
elephants are certainly not native to what we now
call Iraq). But what we do know is that a Jewish envoy
from the Carolingian empire, called Isaac, travelled
to Baghdad and brought the elephant back with him
through Egypt to Porto Venere near Genoa. Isaac and
the elephant spent the winter in northern Italy and
then crossed the Alps in spring 802, arriving in Aachen
in July of the same year.

Why, you might wonder, did the Caliph of Baghdad
want to give Charlemagne such an impressive and
unusual gift? The answer is that the Caliph and Charlemagne seem to have been considering an alliance. This
was a big surprise given how different the two empires
were. In the end nothing came of the plan apart from
the elephant.

Elephants are rather interesting. Abul-Abbas was the
first elephant to have been seen in Europe since Han-
nibal's invasion of Italy over a thousand years earlier,
but that doesn't mean that Europeans had forgotten

about them entirely. In fact, in some ways they were fascinated by elephants, partly because they appear in the Bible. In the First Book of Maccabees, for example, we get this wonderful passage:

> Early in the morning the king rose and took his army by a forced march along the road to Beth-Zechariah, and his troops made ready for battle and sounded their trumpets. They showed the elephants the juice of grapes and mulberries, to arouse them for battle. And they distributed the beasts among the phalanxes; with each elephant they stationed a thousand men armed with coats of mail, and with brass helmets on their heads; and five hundred picked horsemen were assigned to each beast. These took their position beforehand wherever the beast was; wherever it went they went with it, and they never left it. And upon the elephants were wooden towers, strong and covered; they were fastened upon each beast by special harness, and upon each were four armed men who fought from there, and also its Indian driver.

They also had the work of Saint Isidore of Seville who gave a description of the elephant in his *Etymologies* (in between descriptions of the rhinoceros and the griffin):

> These animals were called "Lucan cows" by the ancient Romans; "cows" because they had seen no animal larger than a cow, and "Lucan" because it was in Lucania that Pyrrhus first set them against the Romans in battle. This kind of animal is suited to warfare, for the Persians and Indians, having set wooden towers on them, attack with javelins

as if from a **rampart**. Elephants are very strong in intellect and memory. They proceed in herds; they give a greeting with a gesture, as they can; they flee from mice; they mate facing away from each other; and when they give birth they deliver the offspring in the water or on an island on account of serpents, because serpents are their enemies, and kill them by coiling around them. They carry the fetus for two years, never bearing more than one; they live three hundred years. At first elephants were found only in Africa and India, but now only India produces them.

There is a great account from an English Benedictine monk called Aelfric that draws partly on the Book of Maccabees and partly on Saint Isidore's *Etymologies*:

Five hundred mounted men went with every elephant, and a war-house was built on each of the elephants, and in each war-house were thirty men, fighting with courage and advancing with eagerness. Some people will think it wondrous to hear this, because elephants have never come to England. An elephant is an immense animal, larger than a house, completely surrounded with bones within its hide, except at the navel, and it never lies down. The mother carries the foal for twenty-four months; and they live for three hundred years, if they are not injured, and man can tame them wonderfully for battle. The whale is the largest of all fishes, and the elephant is the largest of all beasts, but nevertheless man's skill may tame them.

For those of you who have read *The Lord of the Rings*, some of this may seem familiar, for this passage provided the inspiration for the moment when Sam first saw an Oliphaunt.

Each of the three great empires of the age took an interest in exotic animals: the Caliphate of Baghdad, led by Harun al-Rashid; the Holy Roman Empire, led by Charlemagne; and the Roman, or Byzantine, Empire, led by Irene, the Byzantine Empress, one of several remarkable women who wielded political power in Constantinople over the years. During his time in office, in addition to the elephant, Charlemagne was given monkeys, a lion from Marmarika, and a Numidian bear. The royal menagerie in Cairo was home to leopards, panthers, elephants, and giraffes, and lines of elephants, giraffes, leopards, and lions regularly processed in front of the Caliph's palace in Baghdad to the amazement of visiting ambassadors. Not to be outdone, the Roman emperors in Constantinople not only put on wild animal fights in the Hippodrome but collected animals too; in 1053, Emperor Constantine IX Monomachos received a giraffe and an elephant from Egypt. Similar collections could be found elsewhere in Europe; in Spain Abdul al-Rahman also collected animals: we know that he had lions, camels, gazelles, and ostriches in his Córdoban zoo.

As we have already seen, Christian writers were fascinated by natural history, just as Roman and Greek writers had been before them. But perhaps the most remarkable book about animals to modern eyes was written in Basra (in what we now call Iraq). It is called *The Case of Animals versus Man Before the King of the Jinn* and describes animals rising up and speaking against human beings. If you know George Orwell's *Animal Farm* you might be surprised to discover that someone else came up with the idea over a thousand years before he did.

The book in which this fable can be found is a scientific encyclopedia that deals with mathematical sciences, natural sciences, the sciences of the soul, and religious sciences in an attempt to combine Greek philosophy with Islamic thought. The fable itself is about seventy men who, after being shipwrecked, find themselves on an island ruled by animals. The King of the Jinns (or genies, as they became known in western translations) convenes a court where a representative from each animal group explains the cruelties they have suffered at the hands of humans, while seven men, one from each nation, attempt to defend themselves. In the end the humans win the case by pointing out that it is only they who have been offered eternal life by Allah, but the King of the Jinns also reminds them that they will go to hell if they mistreat animals. It's not quite the message George Orwell was trying to get across, but it does remind us that the past can sometimes seem surprisingly modern.

And Charlemagne's elephant? You may be wondering what happened to him. So am I. The truth is that he disappeared from the historical records. How and why he died is unknown to us. Another of history's mysteries remains to be solved.

# CHAPTER 31

## *The Vikings*

"IN THIS YEAR, DIRE PORTENTS APPEARED over Northumbria. They consisted of immense whirlwinds and flashes of lightning, and fiery dragons were seen flying in the air. A great famine followed, and a little after that, on 8th June, the ravages of heathen men miserably destroyed God's church on Lindisfarne."

This is the sort of description of the Vikings that you might be used to. It comes from the entry for 793 in the *Anglo-Saxon Chronicle* and gives us all the familiar elements: violence; an unprovoked attack on an undefended monastery; and destruction.

Except the *Anglo-Saxon Chronicle* doesn't mention "Vikings." It refers instead to "heathen men." We are so used to hearing about the Vikings that we might be surprised to hear that the name is misleading. The English usually referred to these deadly sailors as Danes, Northmen, Pirates, or Pagans instead. Nonetheless, I shall use "Vikings" as a kind of useful shorthand, as long as you remember that both "Vikings" and "Anglo-Saxons" are anachronistic terms.

Let's have a look at another account, which comes from Ibn Fadlan's account of his embassy on behalf of the Caliph of Baghdad to the King of the **Volga Bulghars**, written just over a hundred years later.

One of the Rusiyyah stood beside me and I heard him speaking to my interpreter. I quizzed him about what he had said, and he replied, "He said, 'You Arabs are a foolish lot!'" So I said, "Why is that?" and he replied, "Because you purposely take those who are dearest to you and whom you hold in highest esteem and throw them under the earth, where they are eaten by the earth, by vermin and by worms, whereas we burn them in the fire there and then, so that they enter Paradise immediately." Then he laughed loud and long. I quizzed him about that and he said, "Because of the love which my Lord feels for him, he has sent the wind to take him away within an hour." Actually it took scarcely an hour for the ship, the firewood, the slave-girl and her master to be burnt to a fine ash. They built something like a round hillock over the ship, which they had pulled out of the water, and placed in the middle of it a large piece of birch on which they wrote the name of the man and the name of the King of the Rus. Then they left.

This is, in some ways, a much more unfamiliar picture. The writer is a Muslim from what we now call Iraq and he is describing a scene in what we now call Russia. And yet there is much that is familiar as well: the ship burial of the Viking lord; a burial mound (like the Anglo-Saxon ones at Sutton Hoo); and destruction. There is quite a debate among historians about who exactly the Rus were but, leaving that to one side for the time being, it seems pretty clear that what we have here is another description of the Vikings, though not in their familiar territory, or at least not in what we often regard as their familiar territory. But, of course, the whole point about the Vikings is that they were great sailors. They were able to go where their enemies were unable to follow. They went not just to Britain and Ireland but also to Russia and France (where their descendants were the Normans), and to Greenland and North America too.

We mustn't limit our picture of the Vikings. We tend to see them as bloodthirsty, pagan pirates (which is what the word "Viking" means) but that tells only half the story. It seems highly likely that at least some of the Vikings who settled in northern England, for instance, had already been converted to Christianity in Ireland and Scotland before they arrived. In fact, it makes sense to see them as colonists rather than invaders. What is more, the evidence from Viking craftsmanship (of which we have plenty) is that they were far from being simple thuggish pirates. They were also extremely skilled workers of wood, metal, and stone.

One particularly interesting example of their work can be found in the graveyard of a church in Gosforth in north-west England. The Gosforth Cross is clearly a Christian cross but it is also partly carved in the form of the Yggdrasil, the World Ash of Norse mythology. It has carvings of Loki, Thor, and other pagan gods on its sides and is a beautiful, slender cross. But how do we interpret it as historians?

The usual approach is to see the Gosforth Cross as evidence of having your cake and eating it: the Vikings clung onto their Norse gods even after they had officially converted to Christianity. As we have seen from Bede's *History of the English Church and People*, this happened in the case of the Anglo-Saxon King Redwald. The problem with this interpretation is that it is built on the assumption that King Redwald's case was the norm rather than the exception. It also gives little credit to the Vikings; we know they were violent thugs so they can't really have embraced Christianity, can they? That is how the argument seems to go.

The final problem with this interpretation is that it flies in the face of other evidence. One of the greatest of all Norse writers was a man called Snorri Sturluson, who lived in Iceland during the late twelfth and early thirteenth centuries. It is thanks to him that we have the Prose Edda, the most complete record of Norse mythology, the stories of the gods. But Snorri Sturluson was a Christian writing in a Christian country. So what was going on? And what was going on in Gosforth? Was it, as J. R. R. Tolkien put it with heavy irony in his masterful essay on *Beowulf: The Monsters and the Critics*, that the people of this time "could not keep Scandinavian bogies and the Scriptures separate in their puzzled brains?"

The answer, Tolkien suggested, is quite different. He was writing about Anglo-Saxons rather than Vikings but, in this respect, there is little to choose between them. Tolkien explained that it is perfectly possible for a good Christian to write about the pagan past because ancestors mattered to Christians. A Christian can write about pagan honor, courage, and nobility because he is no longer part of the pagan world. But being no longer part of that pagan world does not mean that he has to forget the people of the past, especially when they are his people. The unknown men who carved the Gosforth Cross must have seen in the Cross not the end of paganism but, in some sense, its fulfilment. What was only dimly sensed in the world of the gods was now, when seen in the full light of the Christian story, purged of all its excesses and errors. It was perfectly possible to embrace Christianity and to retain an interest in Norse myths from an earlier era. Maybe that is why the Gosforth Cross was designed as it was.

All of which has taken us a long way from Ibn Fadlan and the Rus, from the Vikings and Lindisfarne, so perhaps we ought to return to the Vikings in England during their pagan days. And while we are there perhaps we should introduce King Alfred the Great.

# CHAPTER 32

## King Alfred the Great

WE HAVE COME ACROSS TWO GREAT POPES—
Leo the Great and Gregory the Great—but only one English
king has ever received the same accolade: Alfred the
Great. So who was Alfred and in what ways was he great?
Like Henry VIII many years later, Alfred was not
born to be king. He was the youngest son of Ethelwulf,
King of Wessex. He had three older brothers but eventually he became king in 871 and what a difficult time it
was. Wessex was one of the greatest of the Anglo-Saxon
kingdoms in the ninth century but it was coming under
enormous pressure from the Vikings.

In 865 a great Viking army invaded Britain and pro-
ceeded to conquer Northumbria in 867 and East Anglia
in 869 before being reinforced and then conquering
most of Mercia between 874 and 877. In 878 Alfred's
forces were surprised at Chippenham by the Viking
forces led by Guthrum, who "occupied the land of the
West Saxons and settled there, and drove a great part
of the people across the sea, and conquered most of
the others," according to *The Anglo-Saxon Chronicle.*

Famously King Alfred retreated to the Somerset
marshes, where he didn't burn the cakes and didn't
disguise himself as a minstrel and creep into the Viking
camp. Sorry, it's a good story but there's absolutely no
historical evidence for it. But he did win a decisive battle at Edington which meant that King Alfred and his
people lived happily ever after.

Or so the story goes.

In reality it was more complex than that. The Vikings
were defeated and Guthrum was baptized but he did

not sail back to Norway or Denmark to live out a peaceful retirement. Instead he stayed in what we can now safely call England, having been given a huge area of land, stretching from London to York and beyond. This part of England which now operated under Viking laws was known as the Danelaw and it's possible to trace its outlines in the place names of the area to this day. In other words, Alfred was a very successful military leader but he certainly didn't rid England of the Viking threat for good. In fact, Viking attacks continued throughout his twenty-eight year reign. So why is he known as Alfred the Great? The answer is that Alfred didn't sit around after defeating the Vikings. He strengthened the English navy, making it more than a match for the Viking invaders, and he rebuilt the defenses of many English towns (or burhs).

He is also seen by many people as the first king of England, though that isn't strictly true. As one Anglo-Saxon kingdom after another fell to the Viking invaders, Alfred's Wessex was left as almost the last kingdom standing. When Mercia and East Anglia were swept away, Alfred had little choice but to go it alone. When he defeated the Vikings he found himself stronger than he could ever have imagined in 871. He didn't control the Danelaw but he certainly controlled all of the South and much of what we now recognize as England. He wasn't quite the king of all England but he wasn't far off.

However, what really made Alfred great were not his fighting skills, nor his political power, but his determination to transform English education. (But, of course, I am a teacher so I'm not necessarily a neutral judge!) Alfred wanted the nobility, the men who were running the country for him, to be educated. He recognized that education, while a good in itself, was also good for him politically. Drawing on what he knew of the great educational reforms that Charlemagne had set in motion, Alfred began his own educational project. He recruited churchmen like Asser, Bishop of Sherborne, to work for him. Asser also wrote a fascinating life of the king. In this book he gives us some interesting facts about Alfred. He tells us, for a start, that Alfred could not read until he was twelve years old, or possibly even older. "However, he was a careful listener, by day and night, to English poems."

This comment is interesting for two reasons. Firstly, Asser goes out of his way to tell us that the young Alfred listened to *English* poetry, rather than poetry in Latin. This may seem like an obvious choice to you, but English did not have the prestige of Latin and so English poetry was often looked down on. Secondly, Asser reminds us that *listening* was important. This was an aural age, when people's listening ability was more finely honed than it is today, which meant that their memories were often better than ours are today. This becomes clear from another story Asser tells.

When Alfred and his brothers were young, their mother promised to give a book of English poetry to the child who could learn the poetry first. Asser tells us that Alfred was spurred on "by divine inspiration" and by the beauty of the illustration he saw on the first page. It's good to know that Alfred liked poetry, but it's also good to know that he liked books with pictures. As you might expect, Alfred learned the poems quicker than his brothers—Asser wouldn't have told the story otherwise—but the point of the story was not to tell us about Alfred's amazing memory or his childhood talents, but to suggest the importance of a particular type of education. Having mastered English poetry, Alfred went on to learn "the 'daily round,' that is, the services of the hours, and then certain psalms and many prayers; these he collected in a single book, which he kept by him day and night, as I have seen for myself." By committing the divine office to memory, Alfred was able to carry out what Asser saw as his divinely appointed task: to be a great Christian ruler.

Elsewhere in his biography, Asser tells us that Alfred collected money to pay for churches in Rome and also "for the universal apostolic pope." What is more, he also set aside land across the kingdom so that poor men "(whether native or foreigner) should be sustained with food, drink and clothes" and ordered that this land should continue to be set aside by his successors "right up to the final Day of Judgement." I haven't checked recently but, sadly, I don't think his successors in the twenty-first century have carried out his wishes in the way he asked.

Alfred was keen to be educated by the best teachers he could find but, more importantly, he wanted his people to be educated too. And he wanted them educated in English, the language of everyday speech. Leading by example, he translated important books like Boethius's *The Consolation of Philosophy* and Pope Gregory the Great's *Pastoral Rule*. In fact, he did more than translate them; he adapted them as he translated, leaving us an unequalled insight into the mind of an Anglo-Saxon political leader. He also commissioned new books, the most important of which was *The Anglo-Saxon Chronicle*, a year-by-year account of the history of England from its earliest days until Alfred's own reign.

Alfred's educational project was limited in many ways. The majority of his subjects remained illiterate in both English and Latin, but what he started was of profound importance. *The Anglo-Saxon Chronicle*, for instance, is one of the most useful sources of information for this period that we have. But the question remains: on the basis of his successes, does Alfred deserve to be considered great? The danger with Alfred, as one historian reminds us, is that we "either take his achievement for granted, or else make him too good to be true." I'll leave it up to you to decide what you think.

# CHAPTER 33

# From Greek to Old English

WE HAVE SAID THAT CHARLEMAGNE'S ELE-phant was called Abul-Abbas, but nobody, not even Isaac who brought him back from Baghdad, seems to have been quite sure what the name meant. According to Einhard, Charlemagne's biographer, it meant Father of the Frown, but he may well have got that wrong. All of which raises an interesting question: which languages were spoken during this era and who understood them?

It depended, of course, on who you were and where and when you lived. The Roman Empire was built upon the successes of the Greeks and so, for many years, Greek was widely known across large parts of the Roman Empire. It was the language of the New Testament, it was the language of Jewish communities outside Israel, and it was widely known by the educated elite of the Roman Empire. It is also very important to remember that it remained the language of the Roman or Byzantine Empire until 1453, long after it had been forgotten in the rest of Europe.

But Latin was in many ways more significant. It was the language of the Roman Empire from North Africa to Britain, from Spain to Italy. It was the language of the people and the language of education. It was the language of the Western Church and the language of the liturgy. After the fall of the Western Roman Empire to the barbarians, it was the Church that kept Latin alive. Irish monks, who had never known Roman rule, used Latin, as did Anglo-Saxons, Visigoths, Lombards, and many others. Gradually this Church Latin, as it is sometimes called, became very different from the language of the people as Latin evolved into early forms of Italian, Spanish, and French. When Alcuin attempted to revive the learning of Latin in Charlemagne's palace school, he introduced the form of Latin he was used to in Northumbria: a formal Latin quite different from the Latin **vernacular** used by many of the Lombards, Franks, and Visigoths among whom he worked.

The barbarian tribes brought their own languages with them. Gothic was particularly important, as were the various Germanic languages that eventually evolved into modern German, Dutch, and English (among other languages). What used to be called Anglo-Saxon is now called Old English by scholars to emphasize its links with the language we speak today, which is why you can't say that Shakespeare (or Dickens or Enid Blyton) wrote in Old English. Old English is a language in its own right, spoken in England between about AD 450 and 1200, when what is called Middle English (which was a mix of Old English and Norman French) took over, before being replaced in turn by what is essentially Modern English from about the sixteenth century. Shakespeare, Dickens and Enid Blyton all wrote in what is essentially Modern English.

Some of the languages from this time have become extinct because they were primarily or completely spoken languages. We know virtually nothing about Vandalic, for example. Other languages, like Gothic, were given a written form and then died out. We have a good chunk of a Gothic Bible but very little else (not that that stopped J. R. R. Tolkien from learning what remained of the language while he was still at school). But Gothic and Old English weren't the only languages to gain a written form; one of the most significant linguistic changes during this era was the invention of Cyrillic script by Saint Cyril (after whom the script is named) and Saint Methodius, the Apostles to the Slavs.

Saints Cyril and Methodius (who were brothers) were invited to preach the gospel by Prince Rastislav of **Greater Moravia** in his people's "own language." This Cyril and Methodius did, but they also created a script in which the language could be written, the script that is now used by Russians, Ukrainians, Bulgarians, Bosnians, Serbs, and many others. When challenged in Venice about their work, Saint Cyril pointed out that "the Armenians, the Persians, the Abasgians, the Georgians, the Sogdians, the Goths, the Avars, the Tirsians, the Khazars, the Arabs, the Copts, the Syrians and many others" already had a liturgy written and celebrated in their own language so why shouldn't the Slavs too? When Cyril died in Rome, Saint Methodius continued his work with full papal support.

But these weren't the only languages of the era. One of the most important, not least because it was the language of the Qur'an, was Arabic. Because Muslims believe that the Qur'an is quite literally the word of God, revealed by an angel in Arabic, they are bound to take Arabic very seriously indeed. Wherever they come from, Muslims learn Arabic. There were two key consequences of this privileging of one language: firstly, it meant that other local languages couldn't compete—we have already seen how in Syria and in Spain, Christians became fluent in Arabic because it was very difficult to get along without it—and, secondly, it meant that translations into Arabic became important.

The great era of Arab translations lasted for little more than a hundred years, from the mid-eighth century onward. These translations were important because they preserved a great deal of classical learning, but not all of it by any stretch of the imagination.

Muslim scholars from this time weren't much interested in history, poetry, or drama. Instead they concentrated on mathematics, science (including alchemy), astronomy, medicine, and philosophy. Muslim scholars translated important scientific and mathematical works but they also made new discoveries too and it is to one of these that we must now turn.

# CHAPTER 34

## *The History of Zero*

WHEN STUDYING HISTORY WE NEED TO ASK the right questions. In fact, sometimes we need to spot that a question needs to be asked at all. Let's take the history of science as an example. Peter Hodgson, who was a lecturer in nuclear physics at Oxford University, once pointed out that, "If we look at the great civilizations of the past, in China and India, in Babylon and Egypt, in Greece and Rome, we frequently find well-developed social structures, magnificent artistic and architectural achievements, imperishable drama and philosophy, but nothing remotely equivalent to modern science." He went on to explain that all the conditions necessary for the growth of science seemed to exist in these civilizations—mathematics, technical skills, writing, an educated class with time on its hands—but, even so, science didn't appear. So our first question is why not?

But in order to answer this question, we need to answer another one first: "What do we have to believe before we can hope to become a scientist?" According to Hodgson, who was a very good scientist himself, we need to "believe that the world is in some sense good, so that it is worthy of careful study. We must believe that it is orderly and rational, so that what we find out one day will still be true on the next day. We must believe that this order is open to the human mind, for otherwise there would be no point in trying to find it. We must believe that this order is not a necessary order that could be found out by pure thought like the truths of mathematics, but is rather a **contingent** or dependent order that can only be found by making experiments."

Once we start asking these questions we can begin to understand why science began to develop when and where it did. It is certainly true that the groundwork for the development of science was laid in Greece by thinkers such as Aristotle. But although the Greeks were great thinkers they did very few experiments, partly because of their understanding of time and the universe. As we saw right back in the first chapter, the Greeks thought that history was cyclical. It went round and round like a Ferris wheel. Aristotle also believed that the stars and planets were incorruptible, that they could not change. He was wrong and so, ironically, one of the greatest thinkers of all time can be said to have held back the development of science for two thousand years.

The big change, according to Hodgson and others, came when people started drawing out the implications of Jewish and Christian beliefs about the world. Jews and Christians believe that God created the universe out of nothing as a gift. It could have been different and so it needs to be studied to reveal its secrets. Because it and people were made by the same God, the universe was also open to human reason. It made sense. It was Judaeo-Christian beliefs about God, time, history and the universe that made science possible. It was because of their religion that Christians made observations and carried out experiments. Even so, it took many hundreds of years before science began to flourish in Christian Europe, so we will content ourselves for the time being with looking at the development of mathematics during our era.

As we mentioned before, the Greeks had no word for zero. In fact, the concept of zero was brought from India by Muslim scholars. If you want to make any progress in math you need to have the concept of zero, so its arrival in Europe was hugely important. Another important mathematical breakthrough was the use of algebra. A mathematician called Muhammad ibn-Musa al-Khowarizmi was the first to work on algebra and his name, in a very twisted Latin version, gives us the word "algorithm." Al-Khowarizmi was one of many Muslim scholars working in the field. In fact, from the eighth to the fourteenth centuries, as Peter Hodgson points out, "mathematics, astronomy, optics, physics, and medicine were far more developed in Islamic countries than in Western Europe." This doesn't mean that mathematical work wasn't going on in Christian Europe. In fact, as we have seen, Alcuin paid a quite a lot of attention to the teaching of mathematics in the palace school in Aachen. In Britain, monks like Byrhtferth of Ramsey were also producing quite complex manuals (in Latin and English) that used mathematics and astronomy to help readers calculate the date of Easter. But the man who probably made the greatest impact on the development of mathematics in Christian Europe during this era was not who you might have expected; he was the pope.

Gerbert of Aurillac had several jobs before he became Pope Sylvester II: he was head of the cathedral school at Rheims then Archbishop of Rheims and then Archbishop of Ravenna. But he is remembered today chiefly for two innovations: firstly, while teaching in Rheims he invented an abacus; secondly, he introduced Arabic numbers into Christian Europe. It is easy to take the numbers we use for granted but just imagine your math lessons if all you had to use were Roman numerals. The fact that you use the numbers you do is down to Gerbert of Aurillac passing on what he had learned from Muslim mathematicians while he was studying in Barcelona.

And that includes perhaps the most indispensable number of all: zero.

# CHAPTER 35

## *The Sound of the Past*

WE HAVE THOUGHT ABOUT WHAT THE PAST might have tasted like and, in various different ways, we have considered what the past would have looked like, but what would it have sounded like?

Like the question of what the past would have looked or tasted like, it all depended on where you lived, who you were, and what you were doing but, nonetheless, we can pick out a few themes, a few *leitmotifs*, running through the grand opera of history.

Most people lived in a wholly **oral culture**. Only a minority of people could read and write, which meant sights and sounds were hugely important. And because they were important, people became very adept at reading sights and remembering sounds. Some of the greatest works of literature ever composed, ranging from *The Iliad* to *Beowulf* to the Arthurian legends, circulated first among storytellers before they were written down.

Since it was predominantly an oral culture, people were also more than capable of listening to and enjoying long speeches from politicians and long homilies from priests, to say nothing of plays and other forms of theatrical entertainment. It is no coincidence that the word "audience" means "one who listens." This is why we have to take rhetoric seriously. Speakers didn't simply stand up and talk off the top of their heads; they shaped and crafted what they were going to say and how they were going to say it.

There were even rhetorical advice manuals like *Ad Herennium* which suggested that "pauses strengthen the voice. They also render the thoughts more clear-cut by separating them, and leave the hearer time to think."

But there is more to the sound of the past than public speaking. Listen to this from the Roman writer, Seneca, who had the misfortune to live above some public baths: "Imagine a quarrelsome drunk, or sometimes a thief caught in the act, or a man who loves to sing in the bath. And then imagine people diving into the pool with a great splash of water. Besides these men whose voices are, if nothing else, at least natural, imagine the hair plucker with his shrill and high-pitched voice continually shrieking in order to be noticed; he's never quiet except when he's plucking armpits and forcing his customer to shriek instead of him." And so he goes on.

Cities were noisy places and some places within those cities were noisier than others. In his *Confessions*, Saint Augustine describes how one of his friends, called Alypius, was dragged unwillingly to a gladiatorial show and how it was what he *heard* that tempted him:

> Alypius kept his eyes closed and forbade his mind to roam abroad after such wickedness. Would that he had shut his ears also! For when one of the combatants fell in the fight, a mighty cry from the whole audience stirred him so strongly that, overcome by curiosity and still prepared (as he thought) to despise and rise superior to it no matter what it was, he opened his eyes and was struck with a deeper wound in his soul than the victim whom he desired to see had been in his body.... [A]s soon as he saw the blood, he drank in with it a savage temper, and he did not turn away, but fixed his eyes on the bloody pastime, unwittingly drinking in the madness—delighted with the wicked contest and drunk with blood lust.

You might be surprised to hear that Alypius later turned his back on the gladiatorial shows and eventually became a bishop and saint.

Saint Alypius would have heard other sounds too: bells calling worshippers to church; hymns and chants in the churches themselves. However, we don't know exactly what early music, including church music, would have sounded like because musical notation only came later. Musical historians and archaeologists have reconstructed ancient instruments but the music they played is more elusive.

However, we do know that what we now call Gregorian chant, which was named after Saint Gregory the Great, developed from earlier forms of **plainchant** and soon spread across the Christian world. This beautiful music forms the basis of all later western music and is still at the center of the Church's life today, which is why the Fathers of the Second Vatican Council wrote: "The Church acknowledges Gregorian chant as specially suited to the Roman liturgy: therefore, other things being equal, it should be given pride of place in liturgical services."

But when Islam burst onto the scene there were some key changes. The Muslim call to prayer is one of the most distinctive features of everyday life in Islamic areas and it was decided very early on that only the human voice should call the faithful to prayer. Christians in Muslim areas were therefore not allowed to use bells to call worshippers to prayer either. Instead they turned to the semantron (a hammer striking wood), which is still very popular in places like Greece and Romania today, or a special stone called the *dewall* in Ethiopia. In other words, different sounds emerged in different places in response to historical events that seemed to have nothing at all to do with sound or music.

Among all this sound and noise and music we shouldn't forget the place of silence. Saint Benedict dedicated two chapters of his *Rule* to silence and so helped influence generations of monks (who, let us remember, were right at the center of the Church and education for hundreds of years): "On account of the great value of silence," he wrote, "let leave to speak be seldom given to observant disciples, even though it be for good, holy, and edifying conversations." And, in another chapter, he wrote that, "Monks should practice silence at all times, but especially at night."

Which seems pretty good advice to me, even today, and not just for monks.

# CHAPTER 36

## A Map of the World

WE ARE USED TO THINKING OF MAPS AS accurate representations of the world but, of course, they are not. Because the earth is a sphere, any flat map is bound to be a distortion, which means that what **cartographers** put at the center of their map tells you as much about their assumptions as it does about the actual center of the world.

Ancient maps are therefore good guides. They are not the sort of guide you would like to take with you on a round-the-world sailing trip, but they are good guides to the way people thought and to the way they saw the world.

So how did they see the world? Well, the first myth to dispose of is the idea that they thought the world was flat. Here is Saint Isidore of Seville in his *Etymologies*: "The globe derives its name from the roundness of the circle, because it resembles a wheel.... It is divided into three parts, one of which is called Asia, the second Europe, the third Africa.... It is clear that two of them, Europe and Africa, occupy half of the globe, Asia the other half by itself."

Isidore of Seville's book provided the basis for what are called T-O maps, a T placed inside a circle, which divided the world into these three parts. It's obviously not a completely accurate representation of the world but what is striking is not only that Saint Isidore knew that the world is round but also that he was fully aware of the vastness of Asia.

It is not just early maps that jolt us out of our preconceptions. Saint Isidore was one of eighteen Doctors of the Church from the period we have covered, so let's look at who the others were and where they came from.

Saints John Chrysostom, Gregory of Nazianzus, and Gregory of Narek were all from what is now Turkey, on the crossroads between Europe and Asia; Saints Basil, Cyril of Jerusalem, John Damascene, and Ephrem were all from Asia; Saints Augustine, Athanasius, and Cyril of Alexandria were from Africa. Besides Saint Isidore, the other Doctors of the Church from Europe were Saints Ambrose, Jerome, Gregory the Great, Peter Chrysologus, Leo the Great, Hilary of Poitiers, and Bede the Venerable. In other words, depending on how you define Turkey, about half of the early Doctors of the Church were from outside Europe.

In a sense this doesn't matter at all. These great saints would have seen themselves as Christians first and foremost, and only secondly as African, Asian, or European. What was more important to them was that they were citizens of a heavenly empire and exiles on earth. But, in other ways, it matters a great deal. Pope Benedict XVI, who worked hard to remind people of the Christian heritage of Europe, once wrote this about the early Church:

> Common opinion today supposes Christianity to be a European religion which subsequently exported the culture of this Continent to other countries. But the reality is far more complex since the roots of the Christian religion are found in the Old Testament, hence, in Jerusalem and the Semitic world. Christianity is still nourished by these Old Testament roots. Furthermore, its expansion in the first centuries was both towards the West—towards the Greco-Latin world, where it later inspired European culture—and in the direction of the East, as far as Persia and India. It thus contributed to

creating a specific culture in Semitic languages with an identity of its own.

People are sometimes surprised to hear about flourishing Christian communities today in Egypt, Syria, Iraq, Ethiopia, India, and China, but in fact the only surprise is that these communities aren't better known. Christianity spread very early to each of these places.

An important question is why it failed to establish itself permanently in all of these areas. There are three main answers. The first is that that Christians never quite managed to convert rulers from outside the former Roman Empire. We have already seen what a difference the conversion of Constantine made to the Church; the conversion of the Chinese Emperor might have made a similarly spectacular difference. The second answer is that the Eastern Churches were largely divided from the Church in Rome and Constantinople by the end of the fifth century. One of the tragic consequences of the theological arguments settled by the great ecumenical councils is that some Christian communities didn't accept the councils' rulings and went their own way, including the Monophysites and the Nestorians. It was Nestorian missionaries who took the gospel to China in the seventh century but, cut off from the Christian mainstream, the Christian communities in China did not survive for very long. A third answer is the growth of Islam. Muslim dominance in North Africa and the Middle East certainly prevented the Church from expanding in these areas.

The map of the world was constantly changing during the period we are covering in this book and the more we look at those changes the more we are forced to reconsider our views of the past and the assumptions we so often work with today. A good example of this is the conundrum of Khazaria.

During the ninth century a king and many of his aristocrats converted to a new religion (at least it was new to them). What was unusual about this conversion, though, was that King Bulan of Khazaria converted not to Christianity nor to Islam but to Judaism.

It is clear that, in most places and at most times during the era we are studying, Judaism was, as Judah ha-Levi put it, the "despised religion." There seemed to be little chance of a Jewish state anywhere in the world until King Bulan decided to convert in about 838.

The presence of a Jewish state in the Caucasus region of what we now call southern Russia during the ninth century raises all sorts of questions. The first are narrowly historical. Given that the Khazars were a semi-nomadic and largely illiterate tribe, we have very little written evidence about them and what we have often comes from outsiders like Saint Cyril, who was sent on a missionary expedition to the area, and Ibn Fadlan, the Islamic emissary from the Caliph of Baghdad. The problem here is not so much bias (though that needs to be taken into account) as the sheer lack of written information. Much the same is true of archaeological and place name evidence, much of which has been wiped out over the years as other tribes and peoples, including the Rus, took over the region.

But the presence of a Jewish state raises wider and arguably more important questions. Given the history of **anti-Semitism**, it is unsurprising that Jewish historians and others have taken a great deal of interest in Khazaria, this exception to the historical rule. Despite this interest, historians are still far from sure about how far or how deeply Judaism became embedded in Khazar society.

The presence of Jewish Khazaria also raises uncomfortable questions for Christian and Muslim historians because it seems as though Khazaria, as a relatively tolerant state, may well have received Jewish refugees from Islamic and Christian areas.

Issues of morality—issues of right and wrong—are sometimes banished from history books as though history could be morally neutral, but we have to guard against value-free history, just as we need to be careful not to create a **triumphalist** view of the past. Historians need to make sure that their own beliefs and convictions don't prejudice or distort their work. However, that doesn't mean that they can stand back from the past as if values were something that could be stripped from the historian's outlook like paint from an old door. As humans we have values; that is part of what makes us human. It is as humans with values that we are able to understand and judge the past. It is because we have values that we can also let the past judge us.

As I have attempted to show in this book, there is much to be celebrated in the history of Christian culture that is often overlooked, but that does not mean that we should overlook the mistakes of Christians as well. One man who realized this was Pope John Paul II, so perhaps it is appropriate to end this chapter with the prayer he prayed at the Western Wall in Jerusalem in 2000 (a prayer later repeated by Pope Benedict XVI):

God of our fathers, you chose Abraham and his descendants to bring your Name to the Nations: we are deeply saddened by the behavior of those who in the course of history have caused these children of yours to suffer, and asking your forgiveness we wish to commit ourselves to genuine brotherhood with the people of the Covenant.

# CHAPTER 37

## *The Elephant in the Room*

WE HAVE ALREADY LOOKED AT ELEPHANTS
in this book but there is another elephant in the room,
a phrase I have been doing my best to ignore. It is now
time to admit that I have been trying to ignore the
Middle Ages out of existence. The elephant in the room
isn't Abul-Abbas but the Middle Ages themselves.

So what's wrong with the Middle Ages? Or Medieval? Or Mediaeval? Why is it that I have refused to
use any of those terms in this book? The reason is that
words matter. The terms we use to describe the past
affect how we understand the past. I'll come back to
this point. But the first reason I dislike the term is that
"the Middle Ages" is so horribly vague. When were the
Middle Ages?

The Oxford English Dictionary (which, it is worth
bearing in mind, is a marvelous resource but not an
**infallible** text) defines the Middle Ages as: "The period
in European history between ancient and modern times,
now usually taken as extending from the fall of the
Roman Empire in the West (c500) to the fall of Constantinople (1453) or the beginning of the Renaissance
(14th cent.); the medieval period; *esp.* the later part of
this period, after 1000."

There are all sorts of problems with this definition.
When were ancient times? When do modern times
start? Did the Middle Ages end in 1453 or during the
1300s? Did they start in the fifth century or the eleventh century? Not even the Oxford English Dictionary
seems sure. Which leads me onto the main reason I
dislike "the Middle Ages." The very concept is a piece

of dismissive propaganda. C. S. Lewis, who was a Cambridge professor as well as an author of wonderful books for children and adults, pointed out that the division of history into an era of classical civilization, followed by the Dark Ages, then the Middle Ages, and finally the glories of the Renaissance is a myth. In fact, it's worse than a myth; he describes it as "a preposterous conception" that was dreamt up by a few humanists who wanted to glorify their own achievements. There was no Dark Age after the Roman Empire fell (partly because, as we have seen, the Roman Empire didn't fall when many people think it did), and the so-called Middle Ages were not a mere preparation for the Renaissance.

So let's return to the words themselves. One definition of "medieval" from the Oxford English Dictionary is: "Exhibiting the severity or illiberality ascribed to a former age; cruel, barbarous." In other words, it is a term of abuse.

So we have a choice: either we rename or reclaim. Or, to put it another way, in order to redeem the Middle Ages from those who would see those wonderful, diverse centuries as "cruel" and "barbarous," perhaps we need to wean ourselves off the term for a while.

On a trip to Portugal, Pope Benedict XVI said that, "Today's culture is in fact permeated by a tension which at times takes the form of a conflict between the present and tradition. The dynamic movement of society gives absolute value to the present, isolating it from the cultural legacy of the past, without attempting to trace a path for the future." If we are to trace a path for the future, we have to look to the past. The danger with terms like "the Dark Ages" and "the Middle Ages" is that they cut us off from the past. They encourage us to be dismissive of history when we should be humble before it. No wonder then that, as one historian recently put it, "we are experiencing more history and more historical change than almost any generation before us, and yet we take virtually no interest in it." If you've got this far in the book, you will know that it doesn't have to be that way.

# CHAPTER 38

# The Return of the Fork or The Problem of When to Stop

IN THE EARLY ELEVENTH CENTURY, A LADY called Maria Argyropoulaina caused quite a stir in Venice. As Saint Peter Damian reported: "She did not touch her food with her hands but when her eunuchs had cut it up into small pieces she daintily lifted them to her mouth with a small two-pronged gold fork." In a society that prized eating with the fingers, Maria Argyropoulaina's dining habits were quite a surprise. But to understand Maria's eating habits we need to take a step back.

Maria Argyropoulaina's marriage to Giovanni, son of the Venetian **doge**, united two important families, Maria's from Constantinople and Giovanni's from Venice, which was still a relatively young city, having been founded by Italian refugees fleeing from the invading Lombards in the sixth century. The marriage was a political union, negotiated after Venice and the Roman Empire united against Muslim sailors who had attacked Bari in Southern Italy. The marriage of Maria and Giovanni was a big event so when Maria used a fork people sat up and took notice.

She was not the first person to have used a fork while eating, of course, but she does seem to have reintroduced the custom into Italy after an absence of many hundreds of years and so she provides us with a useful opportunity to pause and take stock. How much changed over the thousand years we have been studying and how much was as it had always been. Was continuity more important than change or change more important than continuity? As with the fork, had things come full circle?

The answer very much depends on which strata of society you are considering. French historians have reminded us that we need to consider the *longue durée*, those aspects of life that take decades, if not centuries, to change: the climate; agriculture; life expectancy. In many ways, the uneducated rural majority in the year 1000 lived similar lives to their counterparts at the time of Jesus, but everyday life varied dramatically from place to place. Some areas were politically stable but others, especially those threatened by Viking attacks, were not. Life in Islamic North Africa was not the same as life in Christian Britain.

If we look at other aspects of the past we can see that change was clearly much more important than continuity. The religious world had changed out of all recognition, with the Jewish diaspora, the Christianization of the Empire, and the rapid spread of Islam. And because religion was not regarded as a merely private affair, these religious changes made a huge difference to people's lives, affecting everything from their music to their education. It even affected their food (and their cutlery).

Comparing different times leads us to a final question. Where and when should this book end? Britain in 1066 is one possible answer but why should we write about the Norman invasion of England and ignore Norman invasions of Sicily and other parts of Italy in the same century? The conversion of Poland in 966 or the baptism of Saint Vladimir, Grand Duke of Kiev and leader of the Rus in 988 might be other options. Both these dates are hugely significant and not that widely known. But I'm going to end in 1054 with an event that had a profound impact on the whole Christian world and so changed the nature of Christian culture forever.

Although there had been some tension between the Bishop of Rome and the Bishop of Constantinople before the ninth century, they worked with a common purpose more often than not. However, the iconoclastic movement in Constantinople and other events gradually drove a wedge between the Greek-speaking communities of the East and the Latin-speaking communities of the West. Problems came to a head in 858 when the emperor deposed Ignatius, the Bishop of Constantinople, and replaced him with a man called Photius. The pope was asked to intervene and decided in favor of Ignatius. In response, Photius announced that the pope had fallen into doctrinal error and so should be deposed and **excommunicated**. Eventually, Ignatius was reinstated but a great deal of damage had been done in the meantime.

The particular issue that Photius raised was the use of the so-called *filioque* clause in the Creed, *filioque* meaning "and from the Son." It comes from the part of the Creed that describes the Holy Spirit. Since this clause had not been part of the original wording, its insertion into the Creed generated a huge amount of controversy, so much so that in 1054 the Church split in two over the issue, with the pope excommunicating the Bishop of Constantinople and the Bishop of Constantinople responding in kind. It was not the end of peaceful dialogue between East and West but, after 1054, the Church in the East refused to accept the judgments of ecumenical councils called in the West and refused to use the *filioque* clause. What is sometimes called the Great **Schism** had begun.

Pope John Paul II once wrote that, "Europe is Christian in its very roots. The two forms of the great tradition of the Church, the Eastern and the Western, the two forms of culture, complement each other like the

two 'lungs' of a single body.... In the differing cultures
of the nations of Europe, both in the East and in the
West, in music, literature, the visual arts and architecture, as also in modes of thought, there runs a common
life-blood drawn from a single source."

The two lungs continued to breathe after 1054, as
lungs must, but since that date the Christian world has
never been able to draw a deep breath in quite the same
way as it did during its first thousand years.

# APPENDIX A

## Timeline of Dates Mentioned in this Book

**776 BC** The first Olympiad

**44 BC** Julius Caesar becomes dictator for life

**AD 43** Romans conquer Britain

**AD 60** Boudicca's Revolt in Britain

**AD 63** An earthquake damages Pompeii and Herculaneum

**AD 64** Nero's persecution of Christians in Rome

**AD 66** Jewish rebellion against Roman rule

**AD 70** Destruction of the Temple in Jerusalem

**AD 79** Destruction of Herculaneum and Pompeii

**AD 80** Official opening of the Colosseum

**AD 135** The Bar-Kochba Rebellion against Roman rule

**AD 251** Birth of Saint Antony

**AD 258** Pope Sixtus II beheaded

**AD 284** Diocletian becomes emperor

**AD 305** Diocletian retires from office

**AD 312** Battle of the Milvian Bridge

**AD 313** Edict of Toleration issued in Milan

**AD 321** Working on Sunday is made illegal

**AD 324** Constantine defeats Licinius in battle

**AD 325** The Council of Nicaea

**AD 326** Saint Helena's pilgrimage to Jerusalem

**AD 337** Death of Constantine

**AD 356** Death of Saint Antony

**AD 360** Julian becomes emperor

**AD 363** Julian dies

**AD 381** The first Council of Constantinople

**AD 410** Rome is sacked by the Visigoths; Roman legions leave Britain

**AD 431** The Council of Ephesus

AD 450  Pope Leo the Great meets Attila the Hun
AD 476  Rome is attacked by the Vandals
AD 451  The Council of Chalcedon
  527   Justinian becomes emperor
  529   The closing of the school of Athens
  532   Rioters destroy part of Constantinople
  553   The Second Council of Constantinople
  565   The Emperor Justinian dies
  590   Saint Gregory the Great becomes pope
  597   Saint Augustine of Canterbury
        arrives in Britain
  604   Saint Gregory the Great dies
  622   Muhammad flees to Medina
  632   Death of Muhammad
  661   The Umayyad Caliphate begins
  680   The Third Council of Constantinople opens
  712   Toledo captured by Berbers
  732   The Battle of Tours
  750   The Abbasid Caliphate begins
  787   The Second Council of Nicaea
  793   Vikings attack Lindisfarne
  800   Charlemagne crowned emperor in Rome
  802   Charlemagne receives an elephant
  838   King Bulan of Khazaria converts to Judaism
  851   Martyrdom of Isaac in Córdoba
  858   Ignatius, Bishop of Constantinople
        replaced by Photius
  869   The Fourth Council of Constantinople
  966   Poland accepts Christianity
  988   Baptism of Saint Vladimir, Grand Duke of Kiev
 1054   The Great Schism begins
 1453   The end of the Roman Empire
 1944   Vesuvius explodes again
 1980   Earthquake causes damage to Pompeii

# Glossary

*aggregate.* Loose materials, like sand, gravel, or pebbles, used to make cement.

*al-Andalus.* The Islamic kingdom that covered much of what is now Spain.

*alms.* Money (or other gifts) given to the poor.

*anachronistic.* Relating to an idea or object placed in the wrong historical era.

*antiphons.* Psalms, hymns, or prayers spoken or sung in alternate parts.

*anti-Semitism.* Hostility and prejudice directed against Jewish people.

*apocalyptic.* Related to the end of the world; pertaining to the Book of Revelation.

*arbitrary.* Unreasonable, unsupported, based on random choice or personal whim, rather than any reason or system.

*buffer states.* Areas positioned between two larger nations or empires which are at war, or might be likely to go to war with each other.

*carbonized.* Reduced to carbon by heat.

*Carolingian Renaissance.* The revival of learning and culture brought about during the reign of Charlemagne.

*cartographers.* Map-makers.

*census.* An official survey in which the number of people in an area is counted and certain information is collected about them.

*collects.* Short prayers, especially ones spoken by the priest before the readings at Mass

*contingent.* Neither impossible nor strictly necessary so that its truth can only be established by observation.

*creed.* A statement of beliefs, deriving from the Latin word "credo," which means "I believe."

*deities.* Gods.

*doctrinal.* Related to the teachings of the Church or another religious group.

*doge.* The chief magistrate of Venice.

*eloquence.* The use of fluent and well-chosen spoken language.

*excommunicated.* Removed from the community or Church.

*garrison towns.* Towns occupied by troops.

*Greater Moravia.* A state, which no longer exists, in central Europe.

*Hippodrome.* An oval track for horse races, chariot races, and other forms of entertainment.

*illiterate.* Unable to read or write.

*Incarnation.* God becoming man in the person of Jesus Christ.

*infallible.* Without error.

*legislate.* To make laws.

*liturgy.* Public worship.

*martyred.* Killed for one's beliefs, especially religious beliefs.

*Merovingians.* The Frankish dynasty (or royal family) established by Clovis.

*metropolitan.* Relating to an important city; an area overseen by an archbishop.

*Missal.* A book containing the prayers and rites used by the priest in celebrating Mass over the course of the year.

*oral culture.* A culture based on the spoken word rather than on books.

*orators.* Public speakers.

*palisade.* A fence of wooden stakes used as a defense against enemies.

*pantheon.* All the gods.

*papyrus.* An early form of paper made from a plant which grows in the Nile valley.

*patriarch.* The bishop of an important diocese.

*plainchant.* Chanted vocal music which is sung in unison and which has been used in worship from the earliest days of Christianity.

*portents.* Omens or signs.

*precedents.* Decisions that serve as guides when future decisions need to be made.

*pyroclastic.* Made up of volcanic rocks.

*rampart.* A raised defensive area, usually with a parapet or defensive wall.

*reconcile.* To bring together.

*sacked.* Pillaged or plundered from a place which has been captured.

*sacraments.* Outward signs of the hidden reality of salvation instituted by Christ to give grace; there are seven sacraments: Baptism, Confirmation, Eucharist, Penance, Anointing of the Sick, Holy Orders, and Matrimony.

*see.* A diocese, a district under the jurisdiction of a bishop or archbishop.

*schism.* A fundamental break or divide.

*solidi.* Gold coins.

*Torah.* The law of Moses, the five books of the law in the Old Testament, also known as the Pentateuch.

*triumphalist.* Showy pride in the successes of one's own group.

*vernacular.* The local language.

*Volga Bulghars.* A group of people in what is now part of European Russia.

*wergeld* or *wergild.* Blood price or fine to be paid for a crime. It is intended to prevent a feud from turning violent.

# APPENDIX C

# *Afterword*

LIKE ANY HISTORIAN, I HAVE TO BE PREPARED to account for my sources of information and for the ways in which I have used them. However, I am also acutely aware that I can stretch my readers' tolerance levels only so far. So here it is: a relatively brief explanation of what this book has been up to.

But first a few words about the title. Just in case there's any doubt, let me reassure readers that I am not suggesting any equivalence between popes, emperors, and elephants. Elephants are great animals but popes and emperors are of greater historical significance. More justification might be required for the use of "Christian culture" in the title. "Culture," unfortunately, now has a rather restricted meaning but, as Fernand Braudel explains in *A History of Civilizations*, "culture" has a much more distinguished history than "civilization" while also covering the whole gamut of human lived experience.

I have refrained from quoting very much for two main reasons: firstly, because I wanted to keep the book short; secondly, because what I have written is not intended to be used on its own. This book provides the introductory background but it needs to be read in conjunction with other books (including the books of early historians like Tacitus, Eusebius, and Bede). Some specific suggestions are given in the Recommended Reading List.

But what of the approach I have taken to this material? I am largely persuaded by Christopher Dawson that what we should be teaching in schools is the history of Christian Culture (see Dawson's *The Crisis of Western Education* for his argument), though I can also wholly understand why such a proposal should worry some readers. Dawson's argument is complex and I haven't much space, so I shall limit myself for the moment to these words from *The Crisis of Western Education*:

> I see no reason to suppose, as some have argued, that such a study would have a narrowing and cramping effect on the mind of the student. On the contrary, it is eminently a liberal and liberalizing study, since it shows us how to relate our own contemporary social experience to the wider perspectives of universal history. For, after all, Christian culture is nothing to be ashamed of. It is no narrow sectarian tradition. It is one of the four great historic civilizations on which the modern world is founded. If modern education fails to communicate some understanding of this great tradition, it has failed in one of its most essential tasks. For the educated person cannot play his full part in modern life unless he has a clear sense of the nature and achievements of Christian culture: how Western Civilization became Christian and how far it is Christian today and in what ways it has ceased to be Christian: in short, a knowledge of our Christian roots and of the abiding Christian elements in Western culture.

Dawson's books and ideas are now receiving some of the attention they have always deserved. To use a terribly anachronistic word, he is making a comeback. But his is not the final word. In fact, I have taken what might be called a modified Dawsonian approach in this book, partly under the influence of Rémi Brague, winner of the 2012 Ratzinger Prize and professor of philosophy at the Université Paris 1 Panthéon-Sorbonne and at the University of Munich. Brague argues powerfully that Christianity is "a part of the *content* of European culture; it constitutes a part of it alongside other elements such as, principally, the ancient or Jewish heritage." However, more important in his view is the idea that "Christianity, more deeply, constitutes the very *form* of the relationship to its cultural heritage." Brague describes this form (which he calls "Roman") in great detail in *Eccentric Culture: A Theory of Western Civilization* and any attempt to summarize it is bound to do damage to his nuanced arguments. However, to put it simply he claims that Romanity is the essential quality of the European: "To be 'Roman,'" he writes, "is to perceive oneself as Greek in relation to what is barbarous, but also as barbarous in relation to what is Greek. It is to know that what one transmits does not come from oneself, and that one possesses it with difficulty, and only in a fragile and provisional manner." In that sense Christianity is also, by definition, Roman. In Brague's view one can understand Europe only if one understands Christianity, and one can understand Christianity only if one understands what it is to be Roman. Or, to paraphrase Chesterton, the important thing about the countries of Europe is not that they have Roman remains. They *are* Roman remains.

The final writer I want to mention is Norman Davies, whose *Europe: A History* was a massive (and rather unexpected) bestseller. Reading Davies further convinced me that I shouldn't be writing a history of Europe (or even a partial history of Europe). Davies also made me think very carefully about the lacunae of Western Civilization courses and their associated books. But his influence wasn't just negative; he also encouraged me to bite the historical bullet. In *Europe East and West: A Collection of Essays on European History*, Davies wrote "Ultra-specialization is the besetting sin of today's historical profession. Faced with overwhelming torrents of information, historians have taken refuge in ever-narrower subjects, hoping against hope to master the ever-increasing data relevant to ever-shrinking areas of competence." Of course, Davies is not the first to have identified the problem nor the first to have attempted to redress it—Tolkien made a similar point in his 1959 Valedictory Address to the University of Oxford—but the success of his work encouraged me to widen my net, to write not just about western Europe, to set the history of Britain in a wider context, to write broadly narrative history, to avoid the temptation to allow the concerns of the present to dominate the interrogation of the past, to tell a good story.

The idea for this book came after I had spent too long looking for non-fiction to recommend to my students. I had particular difficulty in finding any good history books. One of my colleagues recommended Gombrich's *A Little History of the World* and one of my students *Our Island Story* but since neither book was entirely satisfactory I decided to write my own. It's not entirely satisfactory either. I am sure there are mistakes here, both factual errors and errors of judgment, but that's why second editions were invented. If you spot any mistakes please do let me know.

# APPENDIX D

## *Recommended Reading*

THIS LIST COVERS ONLY A FRACTION OF WHAT could have been included. Consisting mostly of primary sources, it attempts to set out the principal writings which teachers and students may find useful and enjoyable.

*A Mind Intent on God: The Spiritual Writings of Alcuin of York*, by Douglas Dales

*Alfred the Great: Asser's Life of King Alfred and Other Contemporary Sources*, translated by Simon Keynes and Michael Lapidge

*The Anglo-Saxon Chronicle*

*Beowulf*

*The City of God*, by Augustine

*The Confessions*, by Augustine

*Ecclesiastical History of the English People*, by Bede

*The Rule of Saint Benedict*

*The Consolation of Philosophy*, by Boethius

*Institutions of Divine and Secular Learning*, and *On the Soul*, by Cassiodorus

*Two Lives of Charlemagne*, by Einhard, Notker the Stammerer, et al.

*Ecclesiastical History*, by Eusebius

*A History of the Franks*, by Gregory of Tours

*Ibn Fadlan and the Land of Darkness: Arab Travellers in the Far North*, by Ibn Fadlan

*The Etymologies*, by Isidore of Seville

*The Jewish War*, by Flavius Josephus

*The Conquest of Gaul*, by Julius Caesar

*The Letters*, by the Younger Pliny

*Fall of the Roman Republic*, by Plutarch

*History of the Wars* and *On Buildings*, by Procopius

*Early Christian Writings: the Apostolic Fathers*, translated
by Maxwell Staniforth, with revised translations, intro-
ductions, and new editorial material by Andrew Louth
*The Prose Edda*, by Snorri Sturluson
*Lives of the Caesars*, by Suetonius
*The Annals of Imperial Rome*, by Tacitus
*The Aeneid*, by Virgil
*The Desert Fathers: Sayings of the Early Christian Monks*,
translated with an introduction by Benedicta Ward

# APPENDIX E
## Recommended Websites

"The Stanford Geospatial Network Model of the Roman World." Accessed December 30, 2020. http://orbis.stanford.edu/.

"The Early Middle Ages, 284–1000." Accessed December 30, 2020. http://oyc.yale.edu/history/hist-210.

"Benedict XVI Audiences." Accessed December 30, 2020. https://w2.vatican.va/content/benedict-xvi/en/audiences.index.html.

"Internet History Sourcebooks Project." Accessed December 30, 2020. https://sourcebooks.fordham.edu/halsall/index.asp.

"Key to English Place-Names." Accessed December 30, 2020. http://kepn.nottingham.ac.uk/.

# APPENDIX F

## Acknowledgments

EVEN ACKNOWLEDGMENT PAGES HAVE A HIStory. These days authors usually acknowledge the help they have received before pointing out that any errors that remain are entirely their own. So, I was slightly surprised to discover the following at the end of Saint Bede's preface to his *History of the English Church and People*: "Should the reader discover any inaccuracies in what I have written, I humbly beg that he will not impute them to me, because, as the laws of history require, I have labored honestly to transmit whatever I could ascertain from common report for the instruction of posterity."

I too have labored honestly and I too have received help from many people, but I will have to part company with Saint Bede in this one respect: any inaccuracies that the reader discovers are entirely my own responsibility.

I would like to thank all those who have helped me in the writing of this book: my wife and daughters for their patience and tolerance; Gerald Montagu and Ben Kobus for lending me books; Fr Gerry Devlin, Fr Tim Finigan, Michael Hennessy, Brianna MacLean, Julian Murphy, Charlie Strinati, and Robert Teague for helping in a number of different ways; John Riess and everyone at Angelico Press; and especially Chris Doran for reading a first draft of the whole book, making many helpful suggestions, and saving me from a number of mistakes. I am extremely grateful to them and to everyone else who has helped me along the way.

This is how Saint Bede ends his preface: "And in return for the diligent toil that I have bestowed on the recording of memorable events in the various provinces and places of greater note, I beg that their inhabitants may grant me the favor of frequent mention in their devout prayers." It's a great way to end.

Made in the USA
Las Vegas, NV
15 March 2021